Living like a Lord

George Augustus, second marquis of Donegall, in 1800,
by J.J. Masquerier, RA

Living like a Lord

THE SECOND
MARQUIS
OF DONEGALL
1769—1844

W.A. MAGUIRE

THE
ULSTER HISTORICAL
FOUNDATION

For Ian and Caroline

First published 1984 by Appletree Press
and the Ulster Society for Irish Historical Studies
This edition 2002
by the Ulster Historical Foundation
12 College Square East, Belfast BT1 6DD

© W.A. Maguire
ISBN 1-903688-26-4

Printed by ColourBooks Ltd
Typeset by December Publications
Design by Dunbar Design

CONTENTS

PREFACE AND
ACKNOWLEDGEMENTS

Living like a Lord was first published nearly twenty years ago and has long been out of print. I am very pleased that the Ulster Historical Foundation has decided to give it a new lease of life, and hope that a generation of readers who know not George Augustus may have arisen in the meantime to enjoy this salutary tale of a prodigal son who grew up to be a prodigal father.

For permission to use the material in the Public Record Office of Northern Ireland on which this book is largely based, I am most grateful to the deputy keeper and to the following owners and depositors: Messrs L'Estrange and Brett and the earl of Shaftesbury (Donegall papers); Viscount Massereene and Ferrard (Foster-Massereene papers); the marquess of Downshire (Downshire papers); the Honourable Guy Strutt (Strutt papers); the British Library Board (Hertford papers, Egerton MSS); the Harrowby MSS Trust; and Joyce Countess Fitzwilliam and The Brynmor Jones Library, University of Hull (Fitzwilliam/Langdale (Grattan) papers). For valuable material elsewhere I am indebted to the marquess of Donegall (Templemore papers), Staffordshire County Record Office (Fisherwick papers) and Mr John W. Monahan, Castletown Castle, County Carlow (Faulkner papers). I should also like to thank Dr A.P.W. Malcomson for bringing several interesting sources to my attention; and Dr Eileen Black.

The text of this edition is the same as that of the original, apart from a few minor corrections. Opportunity has been taken, however, to revise and expand some of the Notes; and also to adopt a less formally academic style of citing sources. On the subject of sources, the recent publication of the complete Drennan-McTier correspondence (superbly edited by Dr Jean Agnew) has been a godsend to all users of that great mine. Lastly, an index has been added.

Some of the illustrations used here appeared in the first edition; others are new. Those acknowledged to the Ulster Museum are reproduced by permission of the Trustees of The National Museums and Galleries of Northern Ireland (NMGNI). I am indebted to Belfast City Council for permission to include the portrait of the second marquis by Masquerier, which now hangs in Belfast Castle. And I am greatly obliged to Mrs L. Stewart Cox for allowing me to use the portraits of Edward May and his wife; also to Francis Johnston and Alexander Dunbar, for useful information about the May family.

5 July 2002

Edward May junior (*c.* 1783–1819), *c.* 1809; attributed to Thomas Robinson.

May was Lord Donegall's brother-in-law and chief agent, sovereign of Belfast
several times and vicar of the parish from 1809.

INTRODUCTION

THIS BOOK IS ABOUT THE LIFE AND TIMES of George Augustus, sixth earl and second marquis of Donegall, who between the years 1799 and 1844 was the head of the Irish branch of the Chichester family and one of the greatest landowners in the country.

If he had never existed, it would scarcely have been necessary to invent him; for not only was he by no means unique among the Irish landowners of his day in being financially irresponsible and politically unimportant, but he was also in many respects a stock character in contemporary fiction – an overdrawn character, indeed, in every sense of the word. The very fact that he was an exaggerated example of a type, however, makes his career worth looking at as a case study in aristocratic indebtedness. The general outlines of the phenomenon are familiar enough to students of the period and to readers of the novels of the time, but the details of how enormous debts were acquired and how they affected the lives and estates of those who acquired them are often obscure: the curiosities of the sponging house and the debtors' prison; the byzantine proceedings of the court of chancery; the complexities of post-dated bills of exchange and post-obit bonds; the activities of sheriffs and bailiffs; the effects of the landlord's extravagance on the lives and livelihoods of his tenants and the occupants of his estates. All this is particularly interesting in Donegall's case because he was not only the proprietor of large tracts of rural Ulster but also, uniquely, the owner of a major provincial town at a crucial period of its development. The ironic thing is that whereas the first marquis, frequently condemned as the greatest absentee of his day, had strongly influenced the physical shape and appearance of Belfast, his son (often commended as a resident landlord) lost all control of it by his extravagance.

The second marquis of Donegall's extraordinary financial dealings, which provide us with glimpses of the lower life of the upper classes, are the main theme of this essay. His career is interesting also for the affair of his illegal marriage, which was the direct cause of a change in the law of matrimony – Donegall's only influence on legislation, apart from casting his vote in the House of Lords on rare occasions. Above all, this account of his life is intended as an exercise in local history and as an illustration of the way in which the study of a local subject can lead to the treatment of wider themes as the context is established. This is a precise reflection of the way the research itself developed, beginning with a first sight of some intriguing but obscure documents in the Public Record Office of Northern Ireland.

1

THE
PRODIGAL SON

THE FIFTH EARL OF DONEGALL (marquis of Donegall from 1791) married three times, but all his children were born of his first wife, the daughter of the duke of Hamilton. After four daughters, there was great rejoicing when the first of three sons was born in August 1769. The infant was baptised at St James's, Westminster, early in September and given the names George Augustus, in honour of the king, rather than the name Arthur, which was customary in the family. The news of his arrival was celebrated in Belfast not only with the festivities usual on such occasions among the loyal tenantry of a great family, but in a concrete as well as a liquid way, by the gift to the town of an important new building. As the *Belfast News Letter* reported:

> This morning arrived the account of the Right Honourable the Countess of Donegall's being safely delivered of a son and heir, at the earl of Donegall's House in St James's Square, London. An event of such importance to his lordship's family and to the welfare and prosperity of the town occasioned much joy. At noon, the sovereign [mayor], burgesses, and principal inhabitants assembled at the castle, where they were received by Charles Henry Talbot, esq. [the chief agent of the Donegall estates],[1] and after having paid their compliments of congratulation, walked in procession to the ground marked out for an elegant exchange and assembly-room to be built at his lordship's sole expense, when Mr Talbot laid the first stone of that useful edifice in honour of the day… At night, the sovereign, Mr Talbot, and the principal gentlemen met at the market-house on the happy occasion. Drink was given to the populace, great bonfires were made, and the castle and town were splendidly illuminated.[2]

The fifth earl and first marquis was the greatest Irish landowner of his day. Already, through his father, proprietor of an 11,000-acre property at Dunbrody in County Wexford, he inherited from his uncle, the fourth earl, in 1757 estates in Antrim (nearly 90,000 acres), Donegal (160,000) and Down (the townland of Ballynafeigh) totalling not less than a quarter of a million acres, including the whole town of Belfast. Born and brought up in England, sent to school at Eton and to university at Oxford, he was also the greatest Irish absentee of his day. Not only did he not live on his Irish estates, he did not even keep up a house for his occasional visits but instead deliberately bought an estate in England in order to make it his chief residence. As the leading offender he was publicly accused in 1790 of 'draining a manufacturing country of £36,000 a year...' and of having 'raised fines [lump sums in cash paid by tenants in order to get leases] sufficient to impoverish a province, and transported them out of the kingdom to build palaces in another land, where he is unknown or disregarded...'.[3] This was a reference to his activities at Fisherwick in Staffordshire where, after purchasing the property, he had pulled down the old Tudor house and replaced it by a vast palladian mansion with a park of four hundred acres, all designed and constructed by Capability Brown.[4]

The young Viscount Chichester (known from 1791, when his father became a marquis, as Earl of Belfast) was therefore brought up in England. Nothing is known about his boyhood and education except the negative fact that he did not follow his father and grandfather to university at Oxford. He evidently had no interest in the intellectual and cultural pursuits of the former, who collected at Fisherwick an expensive library and rare specimens of natural history (according to one sharp observer, by 1788 he had 'expended £20,000 on books not yet opened, and £10,000 on shells not yet unpacked'[5]). Instead, from an early age he set out to spend his sober father's money recklessly on the turf and at the gaming table. Within a short time of coming of age he was heavily in debt.

The full extent of his imprudence began to be revealed towards the end of 1791, when some of his disreputable creditors took him to court. Lady Newdigate, his father's aunt, wrote this account of an evening she spent with the Donegalls early in the following year:

> I had the whole story of Lord Belfast and a sad one it is; he is indicted
> for perjury and there is to be a big trial before Lord Kenyon on Tuesday

next. I could not make head or tail of the story from his lordship [Donegall] except that the foolish young man had been bamboozled out of £40,000 in the space of nine months by some villanous people who to cover their own iniquity had commenced this suit against him, but Lady Donegall says they have no doubt he will be honourably acquitted.[6]

Lord Belfast always claimed that many of the debts he contracted as a young man, during the nine years between his coming of age and the death of his father, were the illegal demands of unscrupulous people who had duped and cheated him. Many years later, in the course of one of several protracted lawsuits arising out of those early indiscretions it was explained that he had

> unfortunately been made the dupe of gamesters and sharpers who, after persuading him to drink so as to become heated, if not intoxicated, with wine, were accustomed to seduce him to play, and then to obtain from him securities for money which they alleged he had lost to them.

This system, it was claimed, 'was for some years carried on to such an extent as to have become a matter of notoriety and scandal...'.[7]

However dubious some of the claims may have been, debts of not less than £30,000 were admitted and had to be paid. How was the money to be found? It may be useful to say something at this point about the complicated legal means by which families with property tried to prevent it from being wasted by improvident owners and their heirs. From time to time, usually on the occasion of the marriage of the owner or his heir, a legal document known as a settlement was drawn up. Under the settlement two things were arranged for the future which made it difficult – in some cases almost impossible – for an owner to do as he liked. The first was to limit his rights to those of a tenant-for-life only, by specifying who was to get the property when he died and who after that and so on. Usually the heir was one man and usually the eldest son if there were sons, so that the property would not be subdivided each time into smaller and smaller fragments. Primogeniture was particularly important in titled families because most titles of nobility were transmitted through the eldest son and needed to be supported by income from the ownership of land. The other limitations affected the income of the tenant-for-life as well as his right to dispose of the property as he liked. Under a settlement trusts were set up to raise money

3

for the support of other members of the family besides the owner for the time being. A widow was usually provided with an annual income known as her jointure, and younger children commonly got either lump sums (known as 'portions') or annuities. These sums were secured by 'settling' certain parts of the property – that is, by setting aside the rents from particular holdings to pay them when they became due.

What this meant in practice was that none of the settled property could be sold, mortgaged or leased without the approval of the trustees named in the deed of settlement. The trustees were usually relatives or friends of the parties whose interests were being protected, sometimes professional advisers such as lawyers. Once a settlement was made it could be altered only by agreement between the parties or (this sometimes happened when the heir was a minor and could not give legal consent) by a special act of parliament.

The size of a widow's jointure and of the portions for her younger children depended upon her husband's wealth and generosity and upon how much wealth she herself had brought into the family, or how good were her social connections. These family charges, as they were called, were a large item in the expenditure of many landowners and could become a heavy burden. A dowager who inconsiderately survived too long could make things difficult for the succeeding owner of the estate, sometimes for more than one generation (the record in eighteenth-century Ireland was held by the widow of the first earl of Milltown, who outlived her husband by fifty-eight years and drew a large jointure for all that time). When a younger child came of age and claimed a portion, few landowners could simply hand over the cash. Most had to raise the money by means of a mortgage and had to find the money to pay the interest on it out of their own income. There were horror stories among landowners of cases in which so many relatives had been generously provided for that the unfortunate tenant-for-life had only a small remittance for himself and never saw most of the income from his property. Even when things were not as bad as that, family charges made a certain amount of debt inevitable on most estates.

At the time when Lord Belfast's debts made it necessary to find £30,000 in a hurry, the Donegall estates were tied up by a settlement made in 1761 at the time of his father's first marriage. Under the terms of this arrangement the whole of the family's property in the north of Ireland was listed as security for the jointure of the wife who had died in 1780 and for portions of up to £30,000 for the younger children of the marriage (of whom only one now survived). There was also a prudent provision allowing his lordship to give up to £1,000 Irish (about £920 in English money) as a jointure for any future wife. By 1792 he had married for the third time, a young woman nearly thirty years his junior to whom he was devoted. In order to raise the £30,000 needed, it was agreed that a new settlement should be made, and this was done in May 1792. The property in Antrim and Down alone was made the security for a mortgage loan; Lord Belfast was given a private income of £2,000 a year during his father's lifetime – on condition that he should not sell or mortgage it – and the new Lady Donegall was provided with a jointure.[8]

The hope that now Lord Belfast had a regular income of his own he would live within it was quickly disappointed. Two years later, in May 1794, a further settlement had to be made.[9] This time he was being dunned for another £40,000 or more. He could not hope to pay, or even to keep his creditors quiet, without the help of his exasperated father. The new creditors were prepared to wait for their money, provided payment was guaranteed and provided they were paid interest in the meantime. So it was arranged that they were to have assignable debentures, that is, bonds which would be a first charge on the income from the property and which could be bought and sold just like commercial share certificates. Interest at five per cent was to be paid until Donegall died, when his son was to pay the debentures in full. This time most of the estate in County Donegal had to be named as security. The ink was scarcely dry on this document before Belfast was in trouble again, running up debts by gaming and horse-racing and being pursued as before by hungry creditors. This time his father allowed him to go to prison. According to a statement preserved among the papers of one of his creditors, he was in the Fleet prison for debtors in 1794 and was in and out for several years after that. His incarceration was apparently not too rigorous and even enabled him to go on adding to his debts, for he was 'in the habit – with day rules – of going to all public places and all races and fox hunting which were within forty or fifty miles of London for the several years that his lordship was a prisoner'.[10] This extraordinary statement is explained by the peculiar way in which the debtors' prisons were run. Of the two main prisons for debtors in London the other, the Marshalsea, is vividly described by Dickens in the opening chapters of *Little Dorrit* – the Fleet was regarded as the more desirable, partly because of its central location in

Farringdon Street, and partly because a prisoner with friends and connections could arrange to be lodged not in the house itself (the inmates
called it the college and themselves the collegians) but outside. The
Rules of the Fleet, as its boundaries were called, extended beyond the
prison itself to Ludgate Hill and the Old Bailey.[11] The 'day rules' mentioned here evidently extended those boundaries to almost any venue
within reach of London that a well-connected prisoner wanted to visit.
One attraction of this arrangement so far as young Belfast was concerned was that he could go on amusing himself but was immune from
further harassment by his creditors.

It is not clear how long he remained in the debtors' prison on this
occasion. He was still there, or there again, in the summer of 1795
when his release was arranged by Edward May, the Irishman whose
illegitimate daughter Anna he was persuaded to marry in return. Though
May came of a respectable family in County Waterford and later inherited his father's baronetcy, he himself was regarded as anything but
respectable. He is said to have run off with the wife of a Liverpool
merchant to London, where he set up a gaming-house and became a
moneylender and shady attorney; certainly he had dubious dealings
with some notorious sharks in London, and all four of his children
appear to have been illegitimate (the elder son, Stephen, tried without
success to establish a claim to his father's baronetcy, which passed instead to an uncle).

We know little about young Chichester's relations with women, but
the little that is known suggests that he was not a very satisfactory suitor.
At the time he came of age in 1790 he took a great fancy to Cecilia
Ogilvie, the daughter of Emily, Duchess of Leinster, by her second
marriage (the duchess had shocked her friends by marrying her children's
tutor William Ogilvie). Cecilia was only fifteen at the time, a fact which
drew unkind comment from some of her mother's friends. 'Cecilia's
match seems quite a joke,' remarked Lady Torrington, 'seeing her literally in her frock [that is, in the clothes of a young girl] the other day.'
The couple became officially engaged, however, and Lord Donegall
received his prospective daughter-in-law, but then began to talk of delaying the marriage for a couple of years because the girl was so young.
There was further delay about the terms of a settlement, till the duchess took umbrage and broke off the engagement in June 1791.[12] She
and her friends believed that Cecilia had been badly treated and were
now inclined to believe what they had earlier heard, but had not wished

to credit, about Chichester's character and way of life. Here is Mrs Anne Lynch writing to Cecilia's step-sister Lucy Fitz-Gerald:

> How abominable Lord Belfast's behaviour, but thank God he has shown his true disposition so soon, had he worn the semblance of goodness a few months longer our dear Cecilia might have been made by it unhappy for life, as it is dear creature she has only to be thankful she has escaped so happily being married to a dissipated bad man, with such a one my dear Lucy you know she could expect no solid comfort… It is some time ago I was told by letters from London, that the amiable Miss Ogilvie was too good for Lord Chichester – and spoke of him much as your post had done. Such accounts grieved me no little you may be sure, but I still hoped the best, that he was only giddy and did no worse than what I supposed most young men like him did, and that when once he was married all these sort of follies would be heard of no more…[13]

It is reasonable to suppose that the revelation of the young man's debts, then beginning to be known, may have had something to do with the breakdown of the arrangement. The only other reference to early entanglements is to the jilting of a girl named Byng whose brother challenged Chichester but could not get him to fight, according to an anti-Donegall election squib of 1808.[14]

Despite his reputation, as heir to great honours and estates Chichester was a very eligible young man, and his father must have hoped for a suitable match to confirm the position in English aristocratic circles he himself had achieved by his marriage to a duke's daughter and his elevation to the English peerage (as Baron Fisherwick). The marriage to Anna May, about which he knew nothing until the deed was done, was the last straw. Not only did he refuse any further help towards paying recent debts, but as soon as he heard of the marriage he made a will which removed from the disgraced heir's future control every bit of property not included in the settlements and therefore part of his own personal estate. His beloved Fisherwick, the house in St James's Square, the 'unsettled' part of Inishowen (about 20,000 acres), the townland of Ballymacarrett in County Down (bought by Donegall in 1787), the family's portraits by Gainsborough, even the furniture in Belfast, were all to go to his younger son, Spencer Chichester, at that time still a minor.

In addition to the portion of £15,000 that was to come to him under the terms of the 1761 settlement, Spencer Chichester was also to have a sum of £30,000, to be raised out of the lands in County Antrim through which passed the Lagan Canal (recently completed by Donegall at twice that cost). When he came into the property in 1799 the elder brother contested the validity of this charge, on the not unreasonable grounds that whereas his brother was to get cash at his expense, he himself was to have only a large number of worthless canal shares. He paid the interest on the money to his brother for a few years but thereafter the payments ceased. Half a century later the charge was still being described as disputed, by which time the interest alone was said to be £40,000. The final sign of Donegall's displeasure with his elder son was the appointment of the younger as sole executor of the will, a task in which he was to be assisted by the advice of a trustee to guard him, as his father wrote, 'against many embarrassments which the great extent and multiplicity of my concerns and his own inexperience and the unhappy conduct of his brother may otherwise involve him in…'.[15] The remaining property, the Dunbrody estate in Wexford, was settled on Spencer Chichester at the time of his marriage.[16]

The financial relief afforded to Lord Belfast by his marriage to Anna May did not last long. His living expenses indeed were considerably increased as a result, for he now had to support his wife and his wife's relations. We know that he was in the Fleet again in 1797 and, when rescued by a loan from another moneylender, subsequently fled to Ireland to escape his creditors for a time. Since his father would not help him, and since he himself could give no immediate security, he was reduced more and more to borrowing on his expectations by means of post-obit bonds. As the name implies, a post-obit was repayable on the death of the party whose property the borrower expected to inherit. No interest was payable on it before that date; instead, a substantially larger sum had to be repaid, with interest from the time it became due. The multiplying factor depended upon the degree of risk for the lender, in particular the life expectancy of the two parties – actuarial tables were used – and on the desperation of the borrower. In general, post-obits were a dreadfully improvident way of raising cash. An extreme example later in the history of the Chichester family was a nephew of the third marquis who raised about £350 in this way as a young man with faint expectations and who, when he eventually inherited the title but only a fraction of the property, had to declare himself bankrupt for half a million.

The first marquis of Donegall died in January 1799. His elder son's succession to what was still, despite his father's will, the vast bulk of the family's estates was greeted with rejoicing by the London moneylenders into whose hands most of his bonds and debentures had fallen (there was a regular trade in such things, advertised for auction in the coffee houses of the City). It was a day of reckoning, certainly, and the new marquis was at once assailed by a host of creditors, some of whom had been waiting a long time for their money. So many and so formidable were their demands that the whole property was almost immediately put into the hands of trustees, who were to ascertain the validity and amount of the various claims and to establish some order of priority for meeting them, before issuing debentures as security for the payment of sums which they reckoned to be due. The object of the trust was 'to provide a fund for liquidating the demands of persons who really had any fair claim on Lord Donegall' and, at the same time, to exclude those whose pretended claims had originated in gaming and other fraudulent transactions.[17] Donegall later complained, during the course of one of the interminable lawsuits that arose out of these claims,

> that very little investigation took place as to the origins of the claims of the different persons who, at the date of the trust deed held securities... and the consequence was that a great number of debentures were issued to persons whose only claims arose from their having won, or pretended to win, money from him by gaming and horse-racing.[18]

Oddly enough, once in possession of his inheritance, Donegall displayed considerably more prudence and strength of will in evading payment of his debts than he had ever shown during the period when he was acquiring them. He now enjoyed the advantage that as a peer he was no longer liable to be arrested for debt. As one of his legal advisers put it: 'The motive which induced *Lord Belfast* to get out of England in the year 1797 has no operation upon the *marquis of Donegall* in the year 1802 – he knows that his person is sacred...'.[19] The task of the trustees was not an easy one. Not only were the resources in their hands insufficient to pay off the creditors quickly, but Donegall now had a new lease of extravagance which daily added more to his burdens and rapidly diminished his new credit. In November 1800 the solicitor to the trustees, William Lyon, wrote anxiously to the agent in Belfast about the raising of money by taking fines for the renewal of leases:

> I must entreat of you not to lose an hour in sending them, for if the funds should again fail in the bankers hand to pay the interest of

incumbrances and installments of the debentures it will be utterly out
of our power to appease the creditors and they will of course resort to
their original securities against the estates.[20]

The bankers had at first provided the money to furnish the mansion at
West Wycombe which Donegall had rented for himself and his household. So many new creditors appeared, however, that the cautious fin-
anciers became nervous lest their tables and chairs should be seized by
someone else. So, as Lyon reported, everything at West Wycombe was
then sold by public auction 'and his Lordship has not now an article
that he can call his own'. The horrified lawyer went on:

> I will not attempt to describe his mortification and distress under this
> degradation – suffice it to say that he feels himself more disgraced than
> ever he felt himself under any calamity which happened to him in the
> lifetime of his father… his debts are stupendous, and can only be sat-
> isfied by his limiting his expense to little more than a maintenance for
> some years to come.[21]

The hope expressed by Lyon that 'this blow will exalt him to a proper
estimation of the dignity attached to economy, and teach him the les-
son of being superior to demands which he cannot discharge' was, like
all previous such hopes, a vain one.

The best illustration of his relations with his creditors during this
period is his dealings with Isaac Bernal junior, a wealthy London moneylender who had lent him considerable sums in post-obits. The amount
claimed by Bernal was £46,500, plus interest from the date of the first
marquis's death. When the trust was set up, Donegall stubbornly evaded
paying not only his gaming debts but also many such as Bernal's, where
he had actually received only a fraction of the sums claimed. Since the
securities for these debts existed, he could scarcely have hoped to evade
payment entirely. His aim seems to have been twofold: to postpone
payment as long as possible, so that he would have more of his income
to enjoy; and by delay and obstruction to force his creditors to settle for
a good deal less than the face value of their securities. In this campaign
the trust was a useful weapon. When Bernal began to press for payment, Donegall first asked for a proper account:

> Upon conversing with the trustees in whom I have invested my estates
> for the discharge of all my debts, respecting your claim of £46,500
> with interest from the death of my father: I am requested by them to
> ask the favour of you to furnish me with an account of the sums of

money advanced by you to Mr May for my accommodation and the times when they were so advanced in order that the account may be liquidated. I would not trouble you with this if I was in possession of any one document that explains matters between you and Mr May to the satisfaction of the trustees who have no other view than to discharge every debt I owe upon the most honourable principle.[22]

A couple of months later, after Bernal had apparently expressed his dissatisfaction, Donegall wrote:

I must confess after the several letters I have written to you that I am rather surprised at your language to me. I can only assure [you] that I have nothing to do with your debt and you must apply to Messrs Lyon or McGeorge, 150 Bond St [lawyers to the trustees] and dare say everything that is proper will be done but Rome was not built in a day nor can my debts be settled in a day.[23]

And at the end of December 1799, nearly a year after his father's death, he told Bernal to apply to the trustees for information about the debt, as he had nothing to do with it.

Though there was much discussion between the lawyers, and evidently a formal agreement of some sort was reached in March of the following year, by the end of July 1800 Bernal was writing to Donegall in terms of bitter reproach:

…as I have repeatedly told you, and your attorney and trustee Mr Lyon and everyone that has spoken to me about your post obit bonds, so I now repeat again, that I will not take one penny less than £46,500 and interest thereon from 5 January 1799 the day your father died, which is now above eighteen months already, and you always said that I should be the first person that you paid – after your father died, instead of which I shall be one of the last, and as I wrote you in my letter of 24 instant July, so I now repeat to you again that I abide by the agreement you and Mr Lyon proposed to me on 26 March last and which you signed and Mr Lyon and Mr Stevens [Bernal's attorney] witnessed, for payment of those post obit bonds of yours and although I then agreed to it very reluctantly, yet when I agree to any thing I always keep my word.

And as to the £554. 3s. 6d. remaining due to me for what I paid in December 1797 to liberate you from the Fleet prison and to enable you to go to Belfast in Ireland, and on which sum I charge you nothing for interest, nor for my trouble, I expect that you will pay me that sum, and remember the many favours that I have done for you without any gratuity or reward but done solely out of love and friendship and your ungrateful behaviour has been such to me your true friend in all your distress and the only friend that you had in all your distress that I hope, and you should pray to God to forgive you that great sin of ingratitude to me that you have been guilty of.[24]

Despite the repeated assurances of Donegall and his father-in-law Edward May senior (now MP for Belfast) that they were grateful and intended to behave honourably, Bernal now began to harass the Donegalls by seizing their household goods, making it difficult for them to move freely, as a letter from Donegall to Bernal written in November at Brighton reveals:

I have done everything in my power to satisfy your mind and have signed everything you wished and I thought in return that the possession of my property was to be given up, but I find this moment although I have got Mr Stevens discharge in my pocket that he has given fresh orders that nothing shall go off the premises. I really do not know the reason, for Godsake, sir, do not put my family and myself to more disgrace, for we were to have left this tomorrow morning and it will cause nothing but anger from Lady Donegall and disgrace to myself and I do not see how it will benefit you.[25]

Worse was to follow when Bernal seized his racehorses and offered them for sale. Desperately Donegall argued that since the horses belonged to Colonel O'Kelly and not to himself they should not be sold and that if Bernal would only wait until May returned from Ireland he would soon have satisfaction. In the meantime the horses needed their proper exercise, for which they should be sent to Epsom or Newmarket. Donegall was very anxious about them not only because they were his absorbing passion but also because he stood to lose 'a mint of money' if they were unable or unfit to run in January 1801, as he explained to Bernal in a grovelling letter at the end of December:

You probably are not aware of the many troubles you will get into by selling those horses although not my property as I have bets to a very large amount which I must pay whether they run or not, therefore I hope it is not your wish to injure me no more than it is mine to hurt you. Mister Stevens informs me you do not want the horses but wish to be settled with: for Godsake why not settle amicably instead of persecuting me and my friends, it was always my wish.[26]

He also wrote to the auctioneer to warn him that the horses were really O'Kelly's and selling them would cause trouble. Bernal evidently did not believe that they were O'Kelly's and said so in terms which drew protests from Donegall and assurances on his honour that they were, but that he would persuade O'Kelly to relinquish his rights so that Bernal could keep them under execution, if only he would refrain from doing more until after the races. We do not know if the moneylender, who must surely have seen through this ingenuous proposal, was enough of a sportsman to hold off.

Donegall's dealings with Bernal were handled largely by his father-in-law, Edward May the elder. Indeed it appears likely that May, himself a moneylender, was responsible for introducing the two of them to each other. He also borrowed considerable sums from Bernal in his own name but apparently on behalf of Donegall. At any rate these sums – amounting in 1805 to £26,000 – became part of Donegall's debt. After the trustees, May was Donegall's second line of defence against his creditors. Bernal was constantly being told that nothing could be properly settled until May had been consulted or had returned from Ireland or had sorted things out with the bankers. May's letters to Bernal are full of promises and reassurances. 'I shall be in London at the beginning of January,' he wrote on 11 December 1800,

> when my whole business shall be to bring all your affairs to a final conclusion. I have no doubt I shall be able to accomplish every thing to your satisfaction. You have always found me a man of honour and I hope you will continue to do so... I assure you when you mention my neglect to you, you wrong me very much and I believe you do the same with Lord Donegall, who I know means every thing that is honourable and grateful to you and yours...[27]

A month later, on his return from Ireland, he wrote:

> I am just arrived at Wycomb and shall be in town on Friday. I flatter myself I shall be able to settle all affairs between you and Lord Donegall. I wish most sincerely you had not taken violent steps until I saw you, and I request you will now stop, until I fail in concluding matters to the satisfaction of all parties.[28]

He did indeed fail, for at the end of March 1801 he wrote:

> I must request that you will desist from all inimical proceedings against him. I have every expectation of being able to bring his affairs to an

amicable settlement… I am well convinced his Lordship intends every thing that is honourable and just to all his creditors…[29]

In March 1802 May wrote to Bernal's attorney to fix a date for a meeting at which the account would be settled and Donegall would give the best security he could for the punctual payment of the debt. In a postscript he explained what he meant:

By the word settlement I mean, that Mr Bernal shall have debentures signed by Lord Donegall with an order to his trustee to perfect them, or shall have the best securities Lord Donegall and Mr May can give, the sum to be according to the agreement made some time ago between Mr Bernal and Mr May.[30]

A deed of trust was apparently signed, because on 15 April, when about to set off for Ireland, May wrote a reproachful letter to Bernal disclaiming a rumour that he intended to dispute the deed because it had been signed on a Sunday: 'Tell me your authority and I will prove him a designing liar… I hope I am incapable of taking such an advantage…'[31]

He was capable of that and worse, it seems, for there is evidence that along with other London moneylenders such as the notorious John King he traded in his son-in-law's securities on his own account. Whatever happened on this occasion, Bernal again failed to get his money, and in June 1803 commenced a suit against Donegall in the exchequer court in Dublin. The grand total claimed, according to a statement of 1805, was over £87,000. This included May's £26,000 and the interest on the original claim of £46,500 for post-obits.

Meanwhile Donegall went on spending, until his affairs reached a crisis. Lyon reported early in 1802 that:

such of his trustees as are partners in the bank have come to a resolution to apply the rents of his estates in the payment of his debts and to limit his allowance to the mere surplus after discharging the interest of incumbrances and the installments of debentures already granted. Severe as this may, and for a while will be felt, it cannot be dispensed with – the creditors are so offended with the splendour of an expensive establishment while their debts are unpaid, and others daily accumulating that they grow clamorous almost to outrage…[32]

According to Lyon's reckoning his employer had incurred so heavy a debt in the three years since he had come into the title that he would need to devote at least £6,000 a year out of his allowance of £10,000 towards the payment of his 'modern debts'. His credit in England was almost exhausted and his reputation had never been lower. The lawyer continued:

> I am sorry to say that he seems lost to all respect in correct society, and to have foregone that character to esteem which is the ornament of nobility. It is painful to me to hear the bitter reproaches of his numerous tradesmen who have been too credulous and are suffering from the effects of consummate vanity, folly and extravagance in the family now surrounding his lordship[33] [he meant the Mays].

In desperation Donegall decided – or, much more likely, was induced – to flee to Ireland. Such valuables as he had been able to retain or acquire were sent secretly to Belfast to avoid seizure by the creditors, and the family followed shortly after. Lyon wrote:

> How far they [his relatives] will have sufficient influence over his lordship to prevail upon him to immure himself in Linen Hall Street, remains to be proved, but as you write to me in confidence, I am free to express to you my doubts on the subject. I have heard him say that Ireland has no lasting attractions for him... he may be amused for a short time there, but he requires a greater variety than he can meet with in Ireland.[34]

In fact, Donegall was to live in Belfast for the rest of his life.

2

THE TALK
OF THE TOWN

B Y THE TIME HE AND HIS FAMILY – including all the Mays –
moved to Belfast, Donegall's trustees had reduced his allowance
from £10,000 a year to £2,000, had made sure that the income from
his Inishowen estate (the security for the 1794 debentures) went directly into the trust fund, and had made it illegal for him to grant any
leases without their consent. Anything very grand in the way of a residence was thus out of the question, which did not immediately deter
him from negotiating with Lord Dungannon for the lease of Belvoir
Park across the river Lagan, at a reputed rent of £1,500. When this
proved impossible the family installed itself temporarily in a house in
Linen Hall Street (as Donegall Place was then called) belonging to
Thomas Stewart, one of Donegall's law agents. Shortly afterwards they
moved across the street to Donegall House, a large end-of-terrace house
with a side garden, on the corner opposite to what until recent times
was Robinson and Cleaver's department store.

The arrival of the Donegalls and their entourage naturally created a
considerable stir in the society of the town, unaccustomed as it was to
the presence of a resident landlord. Something of that stir can be recap-
tured from the letters of Mrs Martha McTier to her brother William
Drennan and his wife in Dublin. Drennan, a doctor by profession, had
been a notable figure in Irish radical politics in the 1790s. There is a
good deal about local politics in his sister's letters, and of course much
about family affairs. But it is the writer's keen ear for gossip about local
celebrities, and her sharp pen, that make the letters so entertaining to
read and such a good source of information about the Belfast of her

day. And since her mother lived almost next door to the town's leading inhabitant for several years, there are some amusing glimpses of the Donegall household as it appeared to the sober citizenry. Mrs McTier's first impressions were not favourable. The newcomers' arrival, she sourly supposed, would be 'the consummation of gambling, vanity and ruin of our society, already so much changed that in this trading town you might frequently suppose yourself in the midnight revels of nobility', a state of affairs, she added, in which she herself took part 'just as far as I choose with no expense'.[35] After meeting Lady Donegall she wrote next day to her sister-in-law: 'Her ladyship is handsome young and affable but not what in my opinion any man of taste would admire. She is every way transparent'.[36] Even the gift of a carpet, curtains and a 'large Brag table' to help furnish the room in the Donegall Arms Hotel where a genteel card club met was not much approved of, since payment for them was said to be doubtful and already (early April, 1802) his English creditors were after Donegall's furniture. Mrs McTier's neighbours, however, whom she rather despised as giddy-minded and credulous, were apparently less discerning and welcomed the touch of high life the marchioness brought with her. After a ball, concert and supper which went on until four in the morning Mrs McTier wrote of

> our beautiful marchioness, as she is called, stifling the laugh till her white bosom became as rosy as her cheeks, and condescendingly noticing everyone, with the dashy blend of a Mrs Kitty in high life below stairs – so she appears to me, and the whole set abominably minded, but it would be treason in the ears of our merchants' wives to say so.[37]

That Mrs McTier was not exaggerating the hectic pace of Belfast's social life under the Donegalls is borne out by the diary of the sociable Mrs Anne Walker, wife of the commander of the 50th Regiment, which was on garrison duty in Belfast during the years 1802 and 1803. Mrs Walker thought Donegall 'a plain good-humoured man' and the marchioness 'a very handsome good-humoured woman'. She was soon on intimate terms with them and a frequent visitor to Donegall House, the scene of frequent festivities such as this one in June 1802:

> The house was brightly illuminated with coloured lamps, and ornamented with festoons of lamps and flowers. The party assembled was extremely numerous – the dancers only complained of being crowded – and about one o'clock the supper rooms were opened. The supper was extremely elegant, wines choice etc., after this the dancing was

again commenced, till near six o'clock in the morning.[38]

At a Twelfth Night party the following January 'every body in the town' was there, the new drawing room was opened, and about seventy sat down to supper. Even more splendid was an evening in April 1803, when the 'new dining room' was opened and over a hundred guests sat down to another 'elegant supper' of 'ices, champagne etc., etc.' There were also frequent functions in the Assembly Rooms at which Donegall presided as master of ceremonies, not to mention visits to the theatre (the Donegalls had a box, attended everything, and entertained distinguished players such as Mrs Siddons).

Mrs McTier's good opinion was not so easily won. She wrote in June, 1802:

> Our gaiety continues great, and I am almost the only lady who has not waited on and entertained our marchioness – for she accepts from all and in the poorest houses with civility and good humour – though I believe she is horribly tired of being without a flirt, for she is so fond of admiration she would take pains to excite even mine – though she never succeeded.[39]

Gradually, however, Lady Donegall's cheerful good nature, and her demeanour in face of the humiliations which her husband's indebtedness brought upon them both, won her even Mrs McTier's admiration. By the end of 1806, when the affairs of the Donegalls were in one of their periodic desperate crises (which led to their going off to live in Edinburgh for a time), Mrs McTier remarked that Lady Donegall's behaviour in Belfast 'has been unoffending and rather meritorious, charitable, *exact in her own accounts* [in contrast to her husband], chastely proper as to men and their admiration, an attentive mother – never played [i.e. gambled] – and the only failing, which I believe brought bad consequences, was a too great attachment to most worthless parents'.[40]

Donegall's conduct was another matter. When his trustees reduced his annual allowance to £2,000 and prevented him from receiving the rents of the estate himself, or from raising money by granting leases, he was soon in desperation for ready cash. Mrs McTier wrote shrewdly soon after his arrival: 'he says he will not leave this [place] till he is out of debt, in that case he will be in his own prison for life.'[41] He was soon in debt to local tradesmen. As Mrs McTier remarked ironically: 'To such a pitch of improvement is this town got (in some things) that it affords every luxury, and even more than our lord can pay for, whose account for champagne and burgundy the Gordons [a firm of wine merchants in Castle Street] think too high…'.[42] Running up bills with tradesmen was one thing, and normal behaviour for many a wealthy man, but actually pocketing other people's money was another. Donegall had a hunting lodge at Doagh on his County Antrim estate where he maintained a pack of hounds and patronised a hunt. Mrs McTier reported that the members of the hunt had subscribed for claret from Gordons and had put the money 'into Lord Donegall's hand, from which it never could be got'.[43] Unfortunately for his reputation this was not an isolated example of unscrupulous behaviour over money; he also tried to raise cash from his tenants in a way that was not strictly honest. So long as the estate was in trust, no lease was valid unless granted with the consent of the trustees, in which case any cash payment offered by the tenant would go into the trust fund, to be used to liquidate the debts. In spite of this, tenants were offered leases and renewals by Donegall himself early in 1803. A substantial tenant on the estate near Belfast who was, as he said, 'connected with many others desirous of renewing their leases on the estate but having had information that the estate is under trust and that Lord Donegall is not competent at present to renew without the concurrence of the trustees', wrote to the solicitor to the trustees to ask him how far the tenants would be safe in surrendering their old leases (most of which had at least fourteen or fifteen years to run) in exchange for new leases from his lordship. The solicitor, William Lyon, immediately wrote to Chichester Skeffington, the receiver of rents in Belfast, to say: 'I have no hesitation in saying that such of the tenants as surrender their present leases and take renewals from Lord Donegall *without the concurrence of at least two of the trustees,* will take avoidable titles to their lands, and that such renewed leases are liable to be set aside'.[44] Not only was this known to the agent, Thomas Stewart, who had advertised the offer but, Lyon added, Stewart had already had to alter one entire set of leases which had been given without the trustees' consent.

Sometime in 1804 – in what circumstances is not clear – Donegall escaped from his trustees. Perhaps it was the other way around, for many of the early debts were still unpaid, notably the £40,000 (plus interest) owing to the debenture holders under the 1794 arrangement. At about the same time the sober and sensible – but perhaps too scrupulous – Skeffington either resigned or was dismissed, and his place was taken by Donegall's brother-in-law Edward May the younger, whom Mrs McTier described as 'a smart black-guard'. Together with Thomas Stewart (who transacted Donegall's local legal business) May was largely responsible for foiling the attempts of various creditors to seize the family's furniture and possessions by means of a sheriff's warrant, in order to force a sale. The method they used at first was to make themselves fictitious creditors with prior claims and even to carry out dummy sales. Mrs McTier explained to her brother how one creditor failed in 1803:

> By the bye – a little lame fellow came here commissioned by a Jew in London, and while the Donegalls were at Mr Turnley's breakfast laid on an execution on house, furniture, etcetera; without effect of any kind, for Mr May and Mr Stewart had prior ones. The marquis laughed like a simon all the next evening I spent with him at Greg's; where *she* said they must retire to some country place, and eat boiled mutton and turnips.[45]

Though the Donegalls appear to have been cheerful enough on this occasion, there must have been some danger that one of their many real creditors would get his hands on their goods and chattels, for later in the same year, at May's request, the sheriff of County Antrim seized the contents of the house in Belfast and advertised them for sale, whereupon May himself purchased all of them and gave them in trust for his sister. The trust deed survives and lists everything that was bought, from kitchen utensils to horses.[46] The 'parlour furniture' included thirty-one chairs, eight tables, a 'library sopha' and a pianoforte. In the drawing room there were nine tables, two dozen chairs, four 'sophas' and a harpsichord, as well as books and paintings. The linen included five dozen table cloths, three dozen pairs of fine sheets and three dozen pillowcases. Among the tableware was a Wedgwood dinner service and a Colebrookdale dinner and dessert service in gold and scarlet. Outside, eight coach horses, two hacks and a hunter were secured, along with six coaches and carriages of various kinds and in various stages of repair.

Thus assured of the bare necessities of a decent existence, the Donegalls could defy the efforts of the creditors for the time being. According to Mrs McTier, however, the sheriff was in the house again in January 1805, so that Edward May had to be summoned back from Donaghadee shortly after he had set out 'to succour the British parliament' (the elder May was the member for Belfast, nominated by Donegall). His efforts on this occasion do not seem to have been altogether successful, for some weeks later an auction was held. Donegall had made it plain, however, that no one who did not wish to offend him should go and bid. It was apparently well known that these auctions were sham affairs, done to satisfy the letter of the law but stage-managed by the Mays to make sure that no creditor got his money by them.

Less than a year later, in January 1806, Mrs McTier wrote to tell her brother of another and more serious threat:

> That morning the Jew, and his three-legged companion [the sheriff's officer with his staff of office] knocked at Lord Donegall's door, were admitted and instantly set the seal on every article in the house. Yet they [the Donegalls] went to the ball and appeared as usual though I believe there is now no resource, and that all must come *fairly* to the hammer, with the house. Our money'd men have been applied to in vain… though Lord Donegall is looked on as a pigeon for all (even a father-in-law, under the feigned name of Williams) to pluck at, yet his lordship acts so often in the same style, that pity has ceased.[47]

How far Donegall was himself to blame, and how far he was the dupe of his relatives, is hard to say. Mrs McTier obviously did not like the Mays, apart from the marchioness, and she makes more than one reference to their unscrupulous conduct. Speaking of Edward May junior she says, 'he and all his family stick close to this poor man though he hates them – and lately delivered from the base business, it is said another of the same kind has been detected in which the father-in-law was chief partner'.[48] There is no doubt that the Mays did very well indeed out of their relationship with Donegall; the investment made in 1795 in getting him released from prison brought ample dividends not only in cash but also in power and social prestige. Through his son-in-law Edward May the elder – Sir Edward from 1811 – was MP for Belfast for fourteen years, a post in which his son Stephen succeeded him. He and his sons and his son-in-law Thomas Verner practically monopolised the office of sovereign of Belfast, a post worth £500 a year, for thirty years. Edward May junior virtually ran the Donegall estates until his death in 1819, acquiring long leases of excellent building ground in Belfast for next to nothing, not to mention a sixty-one year lease of all the property in Carrickfergus (where he narrowly failed

Elizabeth May, née Sinclair, wife of the Rev. Edward May, *c.* 1809;
attributed to Thomas Robinson

to win election to parliament on the Donegall ticket in 1807) for only
£50 a year, and the valuable salmon fishery on the River Bann for the
same rent and term. He was even appointed vicar of Belfast at short
notice in 1809, being ordained a week before his induction.[49] Of the
four children his marriage to the eldest daughter of a wealthy Belfast
merchant produced, one became a judge and another an admiral. At
the very least, Donegall's constant want of ready cash made him easy
game for those more shrewd and forceful than himself.

After the contents of the house in Belfast had been seized in January 1806, the Donegalls took refuge for a time at Fisherwick Lodge. Mrs McTier reported in March that new furniture had just been bought in there. The final catastrophe in Belfast was delayed for a further nine months but came at last just before Christmas. Mrs McTier gave this description of the proceedings:

> While I write, the bell and crier invite all passengers to bargains at the most noble the marquis of Donegall's – where everything is obliged to be sold, carried off, and the money lodged with the lord chancellor. Yet still there is a shameful juggling over which his lordship seems to preside and even said, he expected none of his friends would bid or appear there… The very splendid furniture of the two drawing rooms, her bedroom, and sedan chair are exempted so as to preclude bidders, and though Lady Donegall before she went away expressed her desire that all might be sold, and all paid, she was no sooner gone than different intimations were authorized both by his lordship and his agents. I suppose to prevent bidders he appears there himself in a very lack a day face, for it is certain that this same sum from the Jews he never touched a penny of and therefore is determined not to compromise with them, but to abide the sentence of the law, which he is taught to believe will be in his favour… She wept for three days and *he* for *one*…[50]

There is a suspicion, nevertheless, that even this humiliation may have been a move in the game which Donegall (or the Mays) played with his creditors. For some time, since the ending of the trust and the resignation of Skeffington, he and his brother-in-law had been receiving the rents and raising money by offering very good bargains to tenants who paid cash for the renewal of their leases. Mrs McTier reports that a substantial tenant named Haliday paid only £700 for the renewal of leases which brought him a thousand a year; and it was rumoured that £30,000 had been raised in this way by the end of 1806.[51] To all outward appearance, however, the creditors had little to hope for. After the furniture had been sold, the house in Belfast was shut up and the Donegalls went off to live in Edinburgh, where for the time being they would be out of the jurisdiction of the English and Irish courts. As Mrs McTier wrote: 'Well if Donegall had (when he could) have taken wise Skeffington's advice, and gone to the continent where he assured him unless he gambled he could not possibly spend more than £4,000 a year'.[52] Perhaps the Mays did not want to go.

Whilst the Donegalls were in Scotland one of the chancery suits which had been rumbling on for several years came to a head. It seems that the creditors who had got debentures from the trustees of the 1794 arrangement – whereby most of the Inishowen estate had been given as security – had received neither payment nor, latterly, even interest on their money. *The Traveller* of 24 March 1807, in a long account of the case, says that the total sum amounted to upwards of £50,000. Several attempts had been made to bring about a sale of the property 'but every measure had been found ineffectual in consequence of the resistance given by the marquis', who had refused to supply necessary documents or to give any information about the leases held by the tenants (a crucial point this, for would-be purchasers). When a sale had eventually been ordered and arranged, Donegall sent word just a few hours before it was due to take place that he had given orders to his agents to resist it 'until there be granted some authority more to the purpose'. The creditors then appealed to the lord chancellor himself to order a sale, and to ask purchasers for a deposit of twenty per cent in case 'his lordship would set up men of straw as bidders for the estates and thus the orders of the court would be frustrated'. This was evidently a well-known tactic, and it is significant that Donegall should have been thought capable of it. On the grounds that he had not yet tried it, however, no precaution against such a move was taken. The chancellor found in favour of the creditors. He thought it desirable that the sale 'should proceed to the best advantage for the sake of the proprietor but it would be his lordship's own fault if it was otherwise. He was residing in Scotland, out of the jurisdiction of the court, but he would be fully apprized of his situation'. The chancellor added that he would never be disposed to help those who were endeavouring to retain their property while leaving their creditors unsatisfied.

There, one might suppose, the wriggling must have ended, but that would be to underestimate the capacity of lawyers to delay matters (especially in the court of chancery) and the determination of Donegall to go on wriggling. A sale was indeed held, but not until two years later, and when the day arrived the property was bought by one William Blacker. Blacker was later to become notable as one of the most successful and progressive land agents of his day (his theories on the management of small farms, published in the 1830s, had a considerable influence on Irish farming and estate management). In 1809, however, he was acting for Donegall in some relatively humble capacity; he was in fact a 'man of straw', bidding to delay the conclusion of the sale.

It was another two years before Donegall finally had to admit defeat. Even then, outright sale was avoided – though only just – by selling leases for 999 years of the manor of Buncrana and part of the manor of Elagh to two tenants named Todd and Harvey, at peppercorn rents.[53]

The Donegalls had returned to Belfast from Edinburgh sometime before the end of 1807, for early in January 1808 Donegall attended a dinner in his honour given by two hundred of his tenantry, at which he was hailed as 'the best and kindest and most liberal landlord in all Ireland'.[54] The sentiment was no doubt sincere, since at a time of booming agricultural prices he was offering long renewals of their leases, at the same rents, in return for very modest sums in cash – a state of affairs which suited the tenants admirably. The return from Scotland was associated with a victory a few months earlier in the court of chancery in Dublin over his old creditor Isaac Bernal, whose claim for £87,500 was reduced to a fraction of that sum. *The Oracle* of 17 June 1807 reported:

> In the case of the marquis of Donegall against Bernal – the lord high chancellor yesterday decreed that an account be taken before the master [of the rolls], of all the money bona fide furnished and that the bonds do stand as security for so much and no more than shall appear to be due on the foot of the account.

This victory must be the one mentioned by Benn as the cause of great rejoicing in Belfast. Bernal, incidentally, was still vainly trying to collect even his reduced award nearly ten years later.[55]

On his return from Edinburgh, Donegall took his family to live at Ormeau in the townland of Ballynafeigh, some distance from Belfast and on the opposite side of the river, keeping Donegall House as a town residence. Ballynafeigh has been part of the city of Belfast for the past century, but in those days it was entirely rural in character and separated from the town by the river (there was no permanent bridge at Ormeau until 1815) – and by low-lying meadows. The house at Ormeau (the word is French for a young elm tree) was then and for another twenty years called Ormeau Cottage. Eighteenth-century maps indicate a country villa, said to have been thatched, which was occupied until 1803 by Lord Dungannon's agent and his family. Presumably the house was enlarged so as to accommodate a large family – Lady Donegall was proud of her seven sons – and its complement of servants (forty or so in number, according to Mrs McTier), and a demesne of nearly two hundred acres was created, but it was always a modest place. Nearby was the home farm, called Hay Park – a name preserved in some of the streets which eventually swallowed it up. Though Donegall was less active than some neighbouring landowners in promoting agricultural improvement among his tenants, he did not escape the fashion entirely and at any rate took an interest in the better farming of his own land. The sheep 'of an improved breed' stolen from Hay Park in 1805, for the recovery of which he offered the large reward of fifty guineas, were probably some of the new Leicesters he had introduced.[56] He also purchased from Astley, the leading English breeder, some long-horned cattle 'of a very superior species'; it is recorded that a beast from this stock, killed in Belfast market, had been fattened at Doagh, on the turnips which were cultivated there.[57]

At Ormeau, Donegall was plagued not only by chancery lawsuits such as the one that diminished his County Donegal estate in 1811, but also continued to be harassed by creditors who tried to seize the family's household possessions. By this time he was expert in all the wiles that could be used to delay or thwart such people. They are all illustrated in the attempts of the Houlditch brothers to enforce payment of a couple of bonds which had come into their hands in the early 1800s.

Edward, John and James Houlditch were partners in a well-known firm of coachmakers at Long Acre in Middlesex and also, it seems, moneylenders. According to the petition which they addressed to the Irish lord chancellor in 1808[58] they had accepted, in order to accommodate Donegall, a bond for £2,000 originally given by him to one William Whaley, which Whaley had subsequently passed to another man, who had passed it to the Houlditches in payment of an account. A second bond for a little over £600, to Sir John Lade, had been acquired in a similar way. Incidentally, if Donegall as a young man had been trying to keep pace with men such as Lade it was no wonder he was soon in trouble, for Lade – a superb rider and coachman, and an expert judge of horseflesh – was one of the leading rakes of the period and a crony of the prince of Wales at his most dissolute. He and his wife Letty, like other fashionable daredevils, took a pride in driving their own carriages in the manner, and with the manners, of the professional coachmen they admired. This accomplishment turned out to be useful, for when Lade had squandered his fortune the prince employed him as coachman.[59] Letty, famous for her foul language, had been the

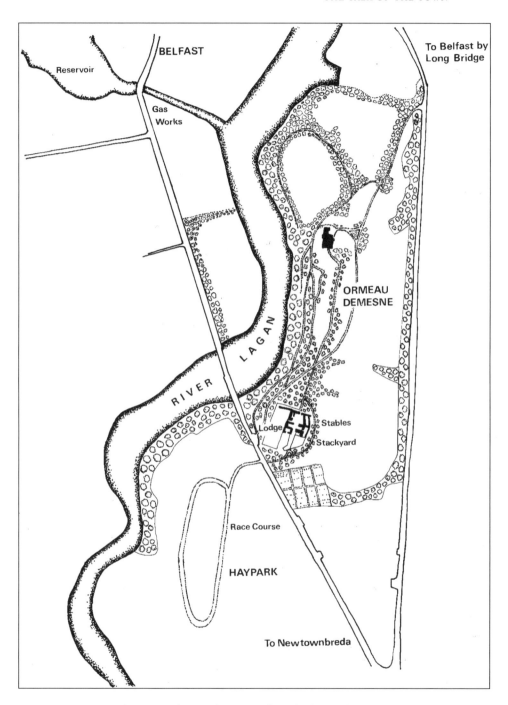

Ormeau demesne and Haypark in 1832, from the first Ordnance Survey map.

mistress of a notorious highwayman known as Sixteen-String Jack, whose career had ended on the gallows.[60] Lade has a place in the history of fashion, too, as the first gentleman to appear in public wearing long trousers. Donegall probably became acquainted with him through the turf, and in particular through the dealings both of them had with the O'Kelly family.

In 1806 the Houlditches obtained a judgment in the court of common pleas in Dublin for the smaller sum, and two years later a judgment for the other in the court of equity exchequer.[61] Payment was repeatedly promised by Donegall and his agents, one of whom, Thomas Stewart, eventually called on the Houlditches at their house in London and, after telling them that the marquis was very anxious to settle with them, offered to use his influence to get them their money quickly – 'upon certain terms' for himself. But though the brothers carried out their part of the bargain Stewart was either unable or unwilling to perform what he had promised, and the Houlditches were obliged to start legal proceedings. Accordingly they obtained an execution (a court order to seize the debtor's belongings) for the smaller bond and delivered it to the high sheriff for County Antrim to put into effect. To make sure that nothing went wrong, John Houlditch went to Belfast himself, where he delivered to the same official an execution for the bond for £2,000.

While in Belfast, Houlditch found out all he could about Donegall's means. 'The said marquis,' he claimed, was possessed of a house in Belfast 'furnished in an expensive and splendid manner well suited to his rank and fortune'; that he was also possessed of 'a great quantity of silver plate which he used at his table and for other purposes'; and that he kept 'a great number of horses and carriages attended by a suitable retinue of servants'. All this was worth several thousand pounds more than the sums owing on the two bonds.

In addition to the house in Belfast, Houlditch discovered that Donegall had two other houses in County Antrim, one at Ballysavage and the other at Doagh, 'each of which houses is well furnished and has a demesne attached to it well stocked with cattle'. These houses were said to contain 'a great quantity of splendid and valuable furniture', and the land to carry many horses, cows, sheep and pigs, along with hay and corn in stacks. At Doagh there were a number of hunters and a pack of hounds, for Fisherwick Lodge was the kennels for the Doagh hunt. The point, so far as Houlditch was concerned, was that the stock and contents of the two places were more than ample, if sold, to settle what was owing on his bonds. In County Down, furthermore, there was the house at Ormeau, elegantly furnished and with a well-stocked demesne.

Estimating his creditor's resources to pay was one thing, getting the sheriff to seize the goods and sell them quite another. Houlditch asserts that on his arrival in Belfast he was told:

> that it would be extremely difficult for him to prevail on the sheriff of the county of Antrim to levy the amount of an execution that might be delivered against the goods of the said marquis, for that besides the influence of said marquis and his agents over the persons immediately concerned in the execution of writs in said county a number of expedients some of which are hereinafter stated and all of which your suppliants charge to have been collusive and grossly fraudulent had been resorted to in order to protect the property of said marquis from the demands of his creditors…[62]

Houlditch then went on to tell how when one of his writs and some belonging to other creditors had been placed in the sheriff's hands and the furniture of Donegall House had been seized, a clergyman named Wolseley had appeared, claiming the goods as his property.[63] The sheriff had held an inquiry, at which a jury had decided that Wolseley was indeed the rightful owner. This inquiry, Houlditch asserted, was a bogus one, held to satisfy the sheriff's conscience but in collusion with Donegall to help him evade the demands of his creditors. The proof of this was that Wolseley – a mere curate – was without the means to have bought a lot of expensive furniture with his own money and to have hired or lent it afterwards to Donegall, as he claimed to have done. It also turned out that at the sheriff's inquiry Wolseley had been represented by Stewart and Macartney, the marquis's law agents.

Convinced by his enquiries that he knew enough to expose Donegall's fraudulent conduct, Houlditch determined to do so 'and thereby make his property amenable, as in justice it ought to be, to the payment of his debts'. His first step was to obtain fresh writs against Donegall's goods which were to be delivered to the sheriffs of both County Antrim and County Down. News of this shrewd move alarmed the marquis, who executed a bond for £3,000 to his agent Stewart, had a judgment entered on it and an execution immediately issued which was delivered to the Antrim sheriff on the same day as Houlditch's writ – though not,

Houlditch claimed, before his. At this point, according to Houlditch, Donegall 'tampered with the said sheriff or his under-sheriff not to execute the last mentioned writ'. The under-sheriff told Houlditch it might not be safe for him to sell the goods, since they had been claimed by others, and declined to do so unless Houlditch would indemnify him. When Houlditch offered an ample security of £15,000 the harassed official agreed. Later, however, he was induced by a similar indemnity on the marquis's behalf, or by some other means, to adopt delaying tactics. Another local jury, summoned by the sheriff, found that the goods in question belonged not to the marquis but to Wolseley. A less determined man than Houlditch might have given up. Instead, Houlditch decided to take an action against the Antrim sheriff for collusion and misconduct.

On the County Down side of the River Lagan the unfortunate Houlditch had no better luck with the local minions of the law. When the under-sheriff received the execution he privately told Donegall about it before making any attempt to seize the goods. This gave time to remove most of the property in the house at Ormeau. Furthermore, having sent word of the time when he intended to arrive, he found the place locked up, but made a show of doing his duty by seizing the cattle in the demesne. Even this, however, was a sham, for on enquiry every horse and cow – and all the hay and corn, and even the farm implements – were found by a local jury not to belong to the marquis at all, but to a man named Ashley who kindly let his lordship have the use of them. Thwarted here too, Houlditch began an action against the sheriff of Down.

At this point, lest Houlditch should succeed in making the local sheriffs do their duty, Donegall sought an injunction from the exchequer court in Dublin to restrain or at least delay further proceedings. The bill that was filed in Dublin was cleverly directed not against John Houlditch – who was in Ireland and could have appeared in court to answer it – but against his two brothers in London and against William Whaley, the original creditor for the larger of the two bonds. Whaley, of course, had long since ceased to have any interest in the matter; not only that, but (as Donegall knew very well) he had been for several years past a prisoner of war in France and was therefore guaranteed not to answer the court's summons. By this neat piece of legal chicanery Donegall got his injunction. The Houlditches were obliged, as a last resort, to appeal to the Irish lord chancellor in the petition which tells this extraordinary story, after their personal appeals to Donegall and his agents had failed.

The appeal to the lord chancellor accused Donegall, Wolseley, Ashley and Stewart of:

> combining and confederating together and with Andrew Savage es-quire high sheriff of the county of Down and Mr Joseph Fulton his undersheriff and with William Moore esquire, high sheriff of the county of Antrim and Mr James Moore his undersheriff and with Edward May junior esquire, sovereign of the town of Belfast… and with divers other persons as yet unknown to your suppliants[64]

to prevent the Houlditches from getting justice. They pointed out the absurdity of the pretence that although Donegall had originally pur-chased all the furniture in his various houses and the stock in his de-mesnes, and continued to have the unrestricted use of these things, everything that appeared to be his really belonged to someone else. They asserted, furthermore, that Donegall had instructed his stewards at Ballysavage, Doagh, Ormeau and Hay Park to keep two separate sets of accounts, one between him and themselves, the other between them and the fictitious owners. It was also asserted that Donegall had tried to persuade a former steward of his to swear at the sheriff's enquiry that the stock at Ormeau belonged to Ashley, and when the man had re-fused to swear what he knew to be untrue had been reduced to per-suading a common weekly labourer to do it instead.

There can be no doubt that the Houlditch brothers were telling the truth. We already know that Donegall would use almost any means to avoid paying his early debts. What may seem to the modern reader harder to believe is that the sheriffs should have aided and abetted him to the extent they did. Clearly it was this as much as the modest ex-pense that made Belfast a good place for him to live in. It was, however, evidently well known that the local patriotism of Irish sheriffs tended to be stronger than their duty as agents of the law. The economist David Ricardo thought that this was one of the major reasons for the reluc-tance of English capitalists to invest in Ireland for, he wrote, 'if an Englishman lending money to an Irishman could by some easy process oblige him to fulfil his contract, and not be set at defiance by the chica-nery of sheriffs' agents, capital would flow into Ireland…'.[65]

The outcome of the Houlditches' petition is not known. It seems likely, however, that they eventually got their money, for when they and others were pursuing Donegall twenty years later (in a case which went to the House of Lords) these two bonds were not among the debts for which they were claiming payment. Whatever one may think of Donegall's conduct in the affair (and there is no doubt that some of those early debts arose from very dubious transactions) there is no need to feel too much pity for the Houlditches. It is scarcely a coincidence that in Maria Edgeworth's novel *The Absentee*, first published in 1812, the vindictive moneylender Mordicai is a well-known coachmaker with his premises at Long Acre.

3

THE CASE OF THE
DETERMINED DOWAGER

AFTER THE DEATH OF HIS FIRST WIFE in 1780 the first
marquis of Donegall had married again. His second wife died at
Fisherwick in September 1789, less than a year after their marriage. A
few months later, when visiting friends in London, Donegall met the
young, attractive and intelligent Barbara Godfrey, the daughter of a
Church of Ireland clergyman from County Kerry. He was at once infatuated and married her as soon as he decently could, just over a year

after his second wife's death, when he was fifty-one years of age and his bride twenty-two. He was a devoted husband, so much so that it was believed he would have bequeathed most of his ancestral property to his young wife rather than to his elder son if he had not been prevented from doing so by the entail. Certainly he seems to have done all he could to make sure that she would have a comfortable widowhood if – as seemed likely – she survived him. In 1792 he made arrangements for her to have a jointure of £1,000 Irish a year, secured on rents from the town of Belfast, and an annuity of £600 from the Ballymacarrett property nearby. By the time he made his will three years later he thought these provisions were not good enough for the widow of a marquis (the will actually says just that) and he therefore added another £400 a year from Ballymacarrett and £500 in cash. She was also to have all the jewels in her possession at the time of his death, coaches and horses, and the use of the house in St James's Square for one year. Three years later, when his health was failing, he added a codicil which provided her with an additional sum of £8,000 to enable her to buy and furnish a house of her own. This tenderness extended to his wife's relations: by a second codicil dated 29 December 1798, a few days before his death (he was by then partly paralysed by a stroke and could only make his mark), her sister Mary got a legacy of £5,000.[66]

Her uncle Sir William Godfrey had represented Belfast in parliament for five years as one of Donegall's nominees; and her father's appointment to the rich living of Midleton in County Cork in 1795 (where his £1,800 a year was more than his predecessor got as Bishop of Clonfert) had also been due to her husband. Strenuous efforts were made to advance Dr Godfrey farther in the church, by getting a bishopric for him, but the government in Dublin Castle would not agree, despite Donegall's considerable influence. The viceroy, Lord Camden, wrote to the duke of Portland at the end of 1797 to explain that it was impossible for him to recommend Godfrey, because '…a supposed intrigue between him and a certain countess in Ireland is too much talked of to make the recommendation a proper one…'.[67]

The dowager marchioness, then, was due to receive £1,000 a year from each of her two stepsons. At first there seems to have been no trouble about the payments, despite the elder's continuing difficulties, because the trustees who controlled the disposal of his income made sure that annuities of this sort were paid regularly, while the younger, Spencer Chichester, allowed the rents of Ballymacarrett to be remitted directly to his stepmother. This satisfactory situation came to an end in 1804, however, when Donegall somehow escaped from his trustees, got rid of his scrupulous agent, Chichester Skeffington, and put his affairs into the hands of his brother-in-law Edward May. Skeffington – 'Chitty' to his family – was a younger son of the first earl of Massereene and later succeeded his two elder brothers in the title; he held the post of collector of customs for the port of Belfast and was a respected local figure. The Chichester and Skeffington families were connected by an earlier marriage, so he was also Donegall's kinsman.

When payment of her jointure began to fall behind, Lady Donegall persuaded Skeffington to act on her behalf. He was perhaps sympathetic to the Donegall dowager because his own mother had recently experienced similar difficulty in obtaining payment of her jointure from his eldest brother the mad earl; in 1801, after a debt of £4,000 had been allowed to build up, the dowager Lady Massereene had been obliged to take her son to the court of chancery.[68] The letters which the Donegall dowager wrote to Skeffington between 1804 and 1810 about her plight provide an interesting if rather one-sided view of Lord Donegall's tactics in dealing with his creditors. The young dowager, an intelligent and cultivated woman, had a keen interest in literature and music. Along with some of her well-connected friends such as the duchess of St Albans, she belonged to the leading literary circle which revolved around the banker-poet Samuel Rogers.[69] She and her sister Mary befriended the Irish poet Thomas Moore, whom they first met in 1802 and with whom there was frequent correspondence during the next twenty-five years or so. Moore often visited them at Tunbridge Wells and elsewhere, and Lady Donegall was godmother to his eldest daughter. The volume of *Irish Melodies* published in 1810 was dedicated to her. Since she was well able to express herself, and did so at considerable length in her letters to Skeffington, we cannot do better than quote her own words. By August 1806 she was writing from Worthing:

> Nothing should induce me to trespass so often upon you but the extreme embarrassment of my present situation... I really am in despair – for I literally have been for the last month without a single guinea in the house – and it is no exaggeration when I say that I have been obliged to borrow money from my own servants to pay for the postage of my letters. I can hardly expect Lord Donegall to feel for me (when he has shown so little feeling for himself) and as to his being sensible of the shame of involving me in such distresses I did not expect it from him...

She was so annoyed that she made the first of many requests to Skeffington to start proceedings to take possession of the estate on which her jointure was secured. 'I am further resolved,' she added, 'upon charging him interest upon every shilling which I have any right to demand it for – for he deserves no indulgence from me...' and remarked in conclusion, '...it really is too hard to be forced to suffer all these inconveniences merely that Lord Donegall may have more money to throw away upon his idle pursuits.'[70]

Two days later she wrote directly to Donegall. We know this because his reply – written from Fisherwick Lodge in County Antrim – is preserved among the letters, the only glimpse of the other side of the case and therefore worth quoting in full:

> I received your letter of the 2nd instant which I must confess surprised me beyond measure. My conduct towards you has been such that neither the world or yourself can possibly take notice of except for the sake of calumny which I did not think the dowager marchioness of Donegall capable of. As to the world I hold it extremely cheap as it very often makes free with people's characters it has not the smallest knowledge of. With regard to yourself had I not on every occasion behaved to you as the widow of my father with the greatest respect I should have conceived myself the monster that your letter seems to express I am. But feeling conscious that I do not deserve it but on the contrary that I have expressed my regard and esteem for you in every company where your name has been mentioned, is it likely that I should wish to deprive you of what is your lawful right and what must my feelings be on the present occasion? On the receipt of your former letter I immediately ordered your money to be paid, which I thought had been paid long ago as it was my express order that your jointure should be paid regularly. On enquiry I find the money has been laying ever since in Messrs Beresford and Company's bank, Dublin, of which Mr Skeffington was informed. The other half year is not yet due. Your threats with regard to taking possession of my estate I think on reflection you will give up.[71]

This reads like the letter of a man who sounds honourable enough and rather aggrieved at being thought otherwise. The dowager was not deceived, and indeed her continuing difficulties – and almost everything we know of Donegall's dealings with other people to whom he owed money – show that she was right. Writing to Skeffington from Worthing towards the end of September she had no less cause than before to complain:

> As I have written to you so often lately, I shall only trouble you with a

few lines now, to beg of you in future to direct to me at Tunbridge Wells, Kent, where I propose removing to on Thursday next, the waters having been ordered for my sister, besides which I have found this place so expensive that paid as I am, it would be impossible for me to remain here any longer. But to enable me to leave this place, I have been forced to borrow money from Mr Hoare [the London banker], which if Mr May had kept his word with you I need not have done. But you must be now convinced that neither Lord Donegall nor Mr May have any regard whatever for their promises, and that they have no sense of truth in any of their dealings, which is a harsh thing to say, but it is a fact – and I may justly be allowed to complain, as I suffer so severely from it. I have now borrowed six hundred pounds from Mr Hoare, the interest upon which I shall insist upon Lord Donegall paying when it becomes due. I hope to hear from you that I shall be soon in possession of the estate, which at last will put an end to all these vexations, which the want of honour in Lord Donegall and Mr May has occasioned me.[72]

The money which Lord Donegall had said was waiting for her in Dublin had not been paid. She later mentions that having applied to Beresford's bank for it she found that Beresford 'had not a guinea' of Donegall's in his hands. She now resolved – rather against Skeffington's advice, it seems – to apply to the court of chancery:

I trust you will believe that there is nobody whose opinions would have more weight with me than yours. But in regard to Lord Donegall, my mind is so made up that nothing can turn me from making the application to chancery but his giving you the same power of receiving the rents, and remitting my jointure, as Lord Spencer Chichester has done… His merely saying, however, that he will consent to it will not satisfy me – he must give you full powers to act independently of himself and Mr May and then I shall be content.[73]

Not only were payments always late, but the bills by which they were paid were sometimes protested (the equivalent of dud cheques). Lady Donegall intended to take no chances, and strongly disagreed with Skeffington that the lord chancellor would not be likely to listen favourably to her. She wrote:

If he and Mr May were quite the reverse of what they are, I should have no hesitation in placing the fullest confidence in them – but with the experience I have had of them, and with the characters they but too justly bear in the world, I do not think that any chancellor would refuse to hear my cause… Oh no, believe me in this instance I am a

View of Belfast from the banks of the Lagan at Ormeau, by T.C. Thompson, 1805

NMGNI ULSTER MUSEUM

better lawyer than you are – as I shall prove, if Lord Donegall does not *immediately* comply with the proposition in this letter...[74]

If there was one thing Donegall was good at, however, it was not doing immediately – and often not doing at all – what his creditors wanted him to do. Possibly, too, Skeffington was reluctant to go to extremes, or knew more of the delay and uncertainty which were inevitable in legal action, especially action in the court of chancery. Lady Donegall suspected that he was reluctant to proceed against her stepson (or 'son-in-law' as she called him). She therefore offered to withdraw the matter from his hands and find a lawyer to act for her:

I feel great concern that I have not had the honour of hearing from you, in answer to the last two letters which I troubled you with, as it confirms me in the idea that you have some objection to proceeding against Lord Donegall, which good nature towards me prevents you from acknowledging. I am therefore come to the resolution of freeing you from what must be a very embarrassing situation... I have written to a friend of mine in Dublin, to recommend me a fit person in the law, for undertaking without loss of time my suit against Lord Donegall – for his promises and those of Mr May are nothing, and I can only hope to be paid by taking possession of the estate.[75]

Her resolution was stiffened by the fact that Lord Spencer Chichester, hitherto praised for his promptness, now also began to pay late (he had in fact been forced to sell Fisherwick, where the great house was demolished). Skeffington was not to be dismissed entirely, however, and indeed one suspects that Lady Donegall was simply trying to get him to move at her own tempestuous pace, for she ended this letter by saying, 'though I believe you have made a vow never to write to me again, I cannot help informing you that my address in future will be 51, Davies Street, Berkeley Square.'

Skeffington evidently replied saying that she was mistaken in thinking him reluctant and, since his reply was accompanied by a remittance of £700 and the news that another could be expected soon, her impatience 'to proceed to extremities' diminished. 'And as you so kindly assure me that your feelings towards him do not influence you, and that you would have proceeded against him without scruple, I shall not now think of employing any lawyer…'. She concluded rather archly:

> Hoping and trusting that you will have the goodness not to abandon my cause. I feel shocked at giving you so much trouble – and really ashamed of asking you now to continue your kind efforts for me – but I feel so secure when you act for me that I should be quite at a loss what to do if you *gave me up*…[76]

One cannot help feeling that the dowager was not really the helpless little woman she sometimes claimed to be.

There is a gap in the surviving correspondence for the next year or so. When it resumes in February 1808, nothing has changed.

> I cannot help boring you with my complaints, and expressing my great impatience for the arrival of that remittance which Mr May has so long promised. I should be satisfied to be half a year in arrears, provided I was paid regularly, and if Lord Donegall would but arrange the payment of his proportion of my jointure as Lord Spencer Chichester has done, I should be perfectly satisfied… But then when I consent to this, I expect that the bills shall be dated accordingly – for if they are drawn two or three months (as they generally are) after date, Lord Donegall must recollect that he keeps me so much the longer out of my money…[77]

In October of the same year, invigorated by the bracing air of Brighton and by lack of punctuality on the part of both her stepsons, she was done with compromise.

> I know I was most extremely disappointed to find… that Lord Donegall has only remitted the money for one quarter when four were due to me – and even for that I must wait until twenty-one days after sight. However by his most unfeeling neglect of me he has done me one service which I thank him for. He has so totally extinguished every feeling of regard or consideration for his credit (which I was once foolish enough to be influenced by) that I mean for the future not to leave it in his power to pay me or not, as he pleases, but to apply to the court of chancery, without loss of time, to put me in possession of the estate…[78]

She went on to remark that anyone could see from her marriage settlement and her husband's will how much the late Lord Donegall had attended to her convenience, 'and by the conduct of his two sons, how little his wishes have been fulfilled by either'. A postscript says:

> The day after I got your letter, I came down here to Brighton – where I had been ordered some time before for my health – but want of money forced me to stay in town till I received your letter – and I have now been obliged to leave all my bills unpaid, which I hate doing – for the credit of the family is so bad that I make it a point, when I can, to pay regularly.[79]

Back in Davies Street at the end of the following month, she was still determined to go to the court of chancery if Donegall would not make a proper arrangement. After quoting an extract from her marriage settlement to the effect that she had agreed to accept £1,000 a year in lieu of the rents of certain tenements in the town of Belfast, provided the payments were made quarterly within one month after they were due, she went on:

> Now though it is as clear as day that I have a right to demand my jointure in these quarterly payments, I shall be satisfied not to insist upon that, provided he will… enter into the same arrangement which his brother has done, which will secure the regular payment every half year of my income. If he will not consent to this, he knows what he is to expect, and he must take the consequences.[80]

At the end of January 1809, having been disappointed again in her hopes of full payment, she was anxiously enquiring what answer Donegall had made to her proposition and suspecting that he delayed merely to prevent her taking any steps against him. 'I shall proceed in the same manner as if he had positively refused my proposition,' she concluded.[81]

There is another gap in the correspondence at this point. The next letter, written from Tunbridge Wells in May 1810, reveals that having received no reply to her proposition she had indeed applied – and applied successfully – to the lord chancellor:

> I had the honour of receiving your letter this morning, enclosing one from Mr May to you. In answer to which, I take the liberty of stating to you that Lord Donegall was in my debt one year and three quarters the 25th of last March. I therefore am quite at a loss how to account for the statement which Mr May makes of the arrears which I am now entitled to receive. It was in his, or rather in Lord Donegall's power, to have stopped any action upon my part long ago, by acquiescing in the compromise which I proposed to him last summer, viz: that my arrears should be paid and that you should be empowered to receive my jointure for the future. To this proposition I could obtain no answer. The consequence of course was an application to chancery, which has compelled them to attend to me. And now Mr May has proposed the very terms which he would not give himself the trouble to reply to, when the proposition came from me. He has now however applied too late. I shall enter into no compromise with him. The chancellor has named you as receiver (and you have had the goodness to acquiesce in the nomination, for which I feel myself sincerely obliged to you) and I shall leave the business to take its regular course – and shall stop no proceedings that can tend to place me in future out of the power of Lord Donegall who, since he had the misfortune to lose your good services, has never for a moment attended to any demand of mine or indeed, I believe, to that of any other creditor, but that is no affair of mine.

After remarking that for some years after her husband's death, when Skeffington had been in charge of making the payments, she had received her jointure quarterly, she went on:

> – but from the moment that chancery appoint a receiver, I am aware that I can only expect to be paid half yearly – but I shall be paid regularly – and that is every thing to me, for I cannot bear the perpetual disappointments I have met with myself, or those that have occasioned to honest industrious trades people, for as long as I owe them a shilling I am miserable.[82]

The next letter, written towards the end of the same month, largely consists of the opinion of her lawyer in Dublin on a letter Skeffington had received from May about the matter of payments owing to Lady

Donegall. It appears that before her chancery bill was filed Donegall owed her five quarters (£1,250). Since no payments were made while the case was proceeding, another three quarters had become due, making two years in all. Before any amicable arrangement (which May had evidently proposed) could be made these arrears would have to be paid. In the meantime no payment should be accepted.[83] The trouble was that for the time being she got nothing at all. No doubt Donegall, by now expert in using the law's delays to bring his creditors to reason, hoped that his opponent would have to accept less than she wanted in the way of guarantees for the future. If so, he was disappointed. Writing towards the end of June to Skeffington she reported:

> I have written directions to Mr Kemmis [her lawyer] to proceed without loss of time, in recovering the whole of the sum now due by Lord Donegall to me – and also in adopting such measures as the court of chancery may authorise, in placing my affairs for the future entirely out of the control of either Lord Donegall or Mr May. The sort of compromise which Mr May wished to propose was merely for the purpose of gaining time... In future what ever communications he or Lord Donegall may wish to make must come through Mr Kemmis – for no mediation (not even yours my dear sir) shall save them from the utmost rigor of the law – and this I beg you will have the kindness to inform them – and I think you will not be sorry to get rid of the bore of trying to mediate between two such parties – the one so totally void of feelings of honour or justice – the other, with a spirit, that instead of being subdued by such conduct, only gains strength – and is resolved on *seeing it out with them*.[84]

She had indeed proved herself to be a woman of spirit.

Her next letter was mainly concerned with arrears owed by Lord Spencer Chichester but concluded with this remark: 'As to Lord Donegall and Mr May, the law will soon compel them to pay me – for my proceedings are going on as fast as they can against them. I say *them*, for I always look on Mr May as having more to say to the suit than Lord Donegall...'.[85]

The last letter in the collection, undated but evidently written in August or September 1810, shows that in the end Lady Donegall reluctantly accepted the offer of an arrangement. There is no less spirit in her words than before, but she must by now have become aware how difficult it was – even with a chancery decree in her favour – to compel her stepson to do exactly as she wanted. On the other hand it appears that she had succeeded in forcing him to accept the arrangement she had proposed earlier. She was not one to accept a compromise easily, however, or to let off too lightly May, whom she had blamed throughout. She wrote:

> The letter in which this is inclosed I have written for Mr May to see – for I really think it too bad that he should now propose a compromise which he would not even give an answer to, when it was proposed to him by Mr Kemmis. I feel decidedly against yielding in anything to him – and always feel that it is better for the law to settle disputes - when one has rogues and fools to deal with. However your advice has, as it ought to have, great weight with me – and if you think I may venture to acquiesce in their proposal I shall do so – but I would rather not agree to it, until you know that the money is fairly lodged with your clerk at Belfast – and in the mean time I should think it would do no harm to send the letter to Mr May. You could say, if you pleased, that you would try and prevail upon me to agree to the terms – but that I was extremely incensed against them – and that you thought it would be difficult to turn me from my purpose – and this is no untruth – for except yourself, no one else should prevail upon me to listen to any compromise with such people.[86]

There are no further letters, and the matter presumably ended with an arrangement which proved satisfactory. In any case it is unlikely that Skeffington continued to act for his client after he became earl of Massereene on the death of his brother in 1811. 'Like to a step-dame or a dowager, long withering out a young man's revenue' is Shakespeare's vivid simile for the slow passage of time. Lady Donegall, who was both, lived on to help wither Donegall's revenue for another twenty years.

4

THE GREAT
O'KELLY HANDICAP

O F ALL THE DEBTS THAT DONEGALL CONTRACTED as a young man and tried as an older one to avoid paying, none caused him more trouble and embarrassment than that which arose out of his dealings with the O'Kelly family. O'Kelly was a name well-known in racing circles in England in the eighteenth century. Dennis O'Kelly, an illiterate but handsome and resourceful Irish gambler and adventurer, had come to England in his early twenties to seek his fortune on the fringes of the sporting world. After a bad period when he was reduced to earning what few shillings he could get as a sedan chairman and a billiards marker, and a spell in the Fleet prison (from which he was released by an amnesty at the death of George II), he became a notable figure on the turf. The change in his fortunes came about because he was taken up by Charlotte Hayes, the leading brothel-keeper in London, who lavished money on him and whom he eventually married. With Charlotte's backing and his own shrewd knowledge of horseflesh he made a fortune. Much of that fortune, as well as his place in racing history, was made when he became the owner of the unbeatable Eclipse, whose victory in his first race – at Epsom in 1769 – O'Kelly prophesied with the immortal words, 'Eclipse first, the rest nowhere', which have found a place in *The Oxford dictionary of quotations.* Though Eclipse ran for only two seasons (no other horse of his time could match him, whatever the handicap) he made £25,000 for O'Kelly in stud fees during his long life at the stables at Cannons near Edgware, as well as siring for his owner two Derby winners (Young Eclipse 1781, and Sergeant 1784). Though he soon abandoned the title of count with which he had dignified himself, O'Kelly became known first as major and then as colonel through his association with the Westminster regiment of the Middlesex militia. His other claim to fame, apart from Eclipse, was as the owner of a notable talking parrot, whose rendering of the 104th psalm was said to be O'Kelly's nearest acquaintance with religion of any sort. He died a rich man at his house in Piccadilly in 1787, two years before Eclipse expired at Cannons – where the crowds of people who came to mourn the beast's passing were regaled with a funeral feast. Though rich and successful, the colonel is said to have died a disappointed man because the Jockey Club would not elect him a member.[87]

The O'Kellys, then, were a rackety lot, though they continued to be prominent in the racing world. The colonel's son Philip inherited the stud at Cannons and was carrying on business there as a breeder and trainer in the 1790s, when young Lord Belfast was recklessly indulging his passion for the turf. Relations between these two began in 1792 and 1793, when some mares belonging to Belfast were sent to O'Kelly's stud. Sometime later Belfast paid a visit to Cannons in the company of an acquaintance named William Whaley and purchased a mare, three colts and a filly at a cost of £3,750. Since he had not a penny of ready cash with which to pay this substantial amount (almost twice the yearly allowance from his father) he gave O'Kelly two bonds each for £550 payable at fairly short notice, and a post-obit for £2,650, payable when his father should die and he himself became marquis of Donegall. If he failed to settle the bonds by the agreed date the amount due on them was to be doubled. As for the post-obit, the amount to be paid was three times the total of the original debt, namely £7,950 (later reduced by O'Kelly to £7,350).[88] Perhaps because he knew his client's reputation for unreliability or, more likely, because he and Whaley (who posed as Belfast's friend but seems to have been O'Kelly's) were in league to pluck their victim thoroughly, O'Kelly stipulated that if Belfast did not pay the full amount within a short time of succeeding his father the penalty was to be the doubling of the debt to £14,700. As if this were not enough in the way of security, he also persuaded his eager client to execute to him a mortgage of the Irish estates to which he was the heir. Since Lord Donegall was at that time in good health there was no immediate prospect of O'Kelly getting his money. The enormous size and value of the entailed property made it a safe speculation, however.

During this period young Belfast seems to have been weak-minded as well as reckless, and so was easy game for those who supported

themselves by living off whatever pickings they could find on the grub-
bier fringes of aristocratic life. He always claimed later that O'Kelly
had swindled him. Their mutual friend Whaley was certainly a dubious character, though of good family, and the bond for £2,000 which
Belfast gave to him – and which later ended up in the hands of the
Houlditch brothers – may well have been one of many that arose from
deception and fraud. William Whaley was a brother of the famous Irish
rake Thomas 'Buck' Whaley, who in the early 1790s made a name for
himself at the London gaming tables (on one occasion he lost £26,000
at a single sitting and, when the IOUs he gave proved to be worthless,
had to flee to Italy).[89] William, the younger brother, had had to disappear
suddenly from Dublin in 1792 when accused of the murder of a cab-
driver whom he had struck in the course of a quarrel about the fare.[90] It
was either 'Buck' Whaley or his brother – probably the latter – who
was responsible for swindling the weak-minded earl of Massereene out
of £9,000, by inducing that nobleman to pass in his favour bills for
which no money was received and which his lordship could not afterwards remember. Massereene later made over to Whaley part of his
estate in County Antrim, but after a spell in the debtors' prison succeeded in establishing by a lawsuit that his debts had been fraudulently
incurred.[91] This happened just at the time when young Belfast was
being fleeced. The parallel between the two – who were also kinsmen –
is extraordinary close, with the difference that whereas Belfast's follies
were those of youth Massereene was middle-aged (he was in his early
fifties at the time) and genuinely eccentric if not mad; he had spent
eighteen years in a French prison before the revolution rather than pay
debts incurred there by his own credulity, and later caused a great scandal in his family by leaving all his property to the servant girl he had
lived with in London and had later married as his second wife.

As it happens, we have evidence from both sides of the O'Kelly story.
Philip O'Kelly's papers and those of his son Andrew Dennis O'Kelly
are among the papers of a family named Grattan in a Yorkshire record
office. They include a letter of 1794 to Philip O'Kelly from 'W.W.'
[William Whaley] concerning the signing of securities provided by Lord
Belfast – a letter which illustrates the complexity of the world of credit
in which the penniless heir was living at the time he bought nearly
£4,000 worth of horseflesh:

> After calling twice upon Lord Belfast, I at length saw him. His lordship
> is very much against giving the bond at a shorter date than six months, .

however I got him at length upon my informing him that I would put him in the way of getting the money, to consent to four months, and you are to give him a good filly: he insists however upon your putting the amount of the bill which you have at present against him, into the bond at twelve months, and he consents to pay you the bond which is to be at four months upon his raising the money, in case he accomplished the business in a shorter time than the four months, which I promise you I can do in Ireland for him... The plan which I propose, in case the bonds are prepared, which most likely they are, is for you to give your word you will not call upon Lord Belfast for payment of the bond which is at twelve months, for a month after it is due, unless it is convenient to him to discharge the same. I also propose a note of hand for the bill which he owes you now, as erasures on the face of a bond are ugly things. His note for so small a sum will secure you as well.[92]

The bonds referred to in Whaley's letter may have been those mentioned earlier; since no amounts are given it is impossible to say for certain. As the story later unfolded in the law courts reveals, those original securities were the cause of the trouble that ensued. Belfast was unable to meet the two bonds for £550 when they fell due, so under the penal clause his debt on that score alone was increased to £2,200. Shortly afterwards he was arrested by other creditors and lodged in the Fleet prison, where O'Kelly's son Dennis frequently visited him. The association with the O'Kellys continued after Belfast's marriage to Anna May in 1795, and the younger O'Kelly evidently became an intimate of both. There were further business dealings too, for Belfast became indebted to O'Kelly by taking a lease of some premises at Epsom which the latter owned. Dennis O'Kelly stayed with the new marquis and marchioness in 1799, when they lived for a time at West Wycombe, and accompanied them to Brighton. He even acted as go-between for Lady Donegall in a quarrel with her husband, who had aroused her wrath by appearing to be about to break his promise to put in her father as one of the MPs for Belfast, in favour of another crony (or creditor). Her letter to O'Kelly on this occasion certainly gives an impression of spirit, though exactly what she was threatening to do with herself is hard to make out:

Should Lord Donegall mention a letter I have written to him this day [1 September 1800, from Brighton] and appear displeased at it you may say that I am a woman of determined mind and what I have said shall be done with respect to my never seeing him more if he does not

Anna, marchioness of Donegall, with her son the earl of Belfast,
Mrs May and Miss May; after the painting by J.J. Masquerier, RA
NMGNI ULSTER MUSEUM

The identity of the gypsy and the seated figure are a matter of some uncertainty.
Mrs McTier refers in one of her letters to a sheriff's sale at Donegall House
in 1806 at which the items sold included 'a family group with Mrs May as a
fortune teller to the Marchioness etc., etc.' Yet the fortune-teller is more likely
to be the Marchioness and the seated figure Mrs May. A romantic young woman,
Lady Donegall loved the theatre and enjoyed dressing up; a miniature
dated 1799 shows her in military uniform.

act as a man of honour should do to the greatest villain I ever heard of
[her father's rival for the seat]. He may say that I cannot live without
an allowance. I shall not want it as once away from this house I can
settle myself in a situation from which I cannot be recalled. Do not be
surprised, but my spirits are affected and I am not well, but I would
carry anything into execution as I am completely sick of the deceit of
this world.[93]

THE GREAT O'KELLY HANDICAP

O'Kelly replied three days later, promising that everything necessary to have May returned would be done without loss of time (Edward May was in fact elected in 1800 and continued to be a member for Belfast until his death in 1814). 'But,' O'Kelly added:

> I confidently rely upon your immediately writing an affectionate con-
> ciliatory letter to my poor friend [her husband] whose present per-
> plexities have very greatly affected his health and spirits... Pray re-
> member me most kindly to all my friends with you and believe me to
> remain my dear Lady Donegall your most sincere faithful and affec-
> tionate friend.[94]

This was exactly what O'Kelly was not, according to the writer of an anonymous letter which Lady Donegall received shortly afterwards. 'O'Kelly is not the man he appears,' it ran,

> duplicity is the chief part of his composition. His first aim is, to have
> the reputation of receiving your favours, his second to continue to pay
> his expenses from your husband's pocket. Before the death of Lord
> Donegall's father he and his family were in the greatest distress. Char-
> lotte Hayes [the old colonel's widow] was in the Fleet. I thus have
> cautioned you, wishing to protect innocence, beauty and virtue. I am
> a real friend to Mr May and his family.[95]

The anonymous scribe was right about one thing. The O'Kellys were in financial difficulties at this time, for among their papers is a sale advertisement dated April 1800 for the stud at Edgware. Whatever the cause of the crisis the O'Kellys survived it, for Dennis O'Kelly was writing from Cannons four years later and his father died there in the following year.

To continue the story of the securities which young Belfast had so recklessly given in exchange for horses he could not afford: as soon as Philip O'Kelly had the post-obit in his possession he had proceeded to have it registered in the courts in England and Ireland, thus making Belfast liable for over £14,000 if he did not pay half that sum as soon as he came into his inheritance. When that happy day arrived, however, and O'Kelly began to press for payment, the trustees who had taken charge of the new marquis's tangled affairs obtained an injunction to restrain execution of the judgment of 1794 and to have the account between O'Kelly and Donegall investigated by an impartial referee, on the ground that O'Kelly was claiming far more than he had any right to. The investigation proceeded slowly through the court of chancery, the referee taking until 1804 to rule that Donegall owed only £2,100 and another £1,000 payable on a debenture issued to O'Kelly by the trustees, a small sum in cash having been paid in the meantime.[96] O'Kelly was far from satisfied with this outcome, but proceeded to seek payment of the sums awarded. Meanwhile, however, in collaboration with other dubious and dissatisfied creditors, he had filed charges in another suit in which the chief claimant was a London moneylender with the unlikely name of Inigo Jones – the same suit, incidentally, that the Houlditch brothers pressed with some success more than twenty years later.[97]

Philip O'Kelly's death in 1805 brought a pause of several years in the pursuit. So far as we know his son Dennis – Colonel O'Kelly as he called himself – made no move against his former friend until the year 1814, when he suddenly appeared in Belfast accompanied by a solicitor and demanded payment from Donegall of various sums which he claimed were due to him both on his own account and as administrator of his father's estate. This spectre from the past appearing on his own doorstep must have been an unwelcome shock for poor Donegall, who was being hard pressed at the time from other quarters. He was forced to agree to an immediate investigation in the presence of two local bankers. The outcome of this was favourable to O'Kelly, whose demand in his own right was agreed to be just over £9,000 and in his father's just under £6,000. These sums included amounts for interest and for the dilapidation of the house at Epsom which Donegall had leased from O'Kelly many years before. O'Kelly in fact claimed a further £2,650 for dilapidation but agreed to leave that out of the account, to be settled later. An agreement for discharging the £15,000 was then drawn up and signed on 15 October 1814.[98] Unfortunately it did not specify the items accepted as due on Philip O'Kelly's account, and his son was later to claim that Donegall had agreed on his honour to pay other sums whenever he could.

According to the agreement, the two bankers who had witnessed it were to act as trustees and to pay £3,000 to O'Kelly within six months out of the rents of the estate, provided they had sufficient cash in hand after payment of three prior encumbrances which were listed. When O'Kelly applied for his money, however, he found not only that there were no funds but also that the trustees had resigned.[99] It must have been exasperating at the best of times to undertake such work for a man like Donegall whose affairs were so complicated and whose methods were so devious. An observer remarked: 'He sometimes grows impatient with the rules upon which they act; they threaten to resign the trust, from which they derive no profit and certainly no amusement; and in this sort of vacillation they carry on their proceedings.'[100] To make matters worse, both Sir Edward May and his son Edward were seriously ill (the old man died soon afterwards) and unable to give much assistance. The agreement in any case was probably one of those delaying devices of which the marquis had so frequent need. If so, it did not work for long, for O'Kelly's next move was to revive the former judgment for £14,700 based on the post-obit of 1794. Donegall successfully sought an injunction to restrain O'Kelly from proceeding with this suit, but had to agree to pay him £3,000 and to insure his own life for £12,000 to cover the remainder of the debt.

O'Kelly pressed home his advantage, quite literally, by obtaining an execution against Donegall's possessions at Ormeau. It was reported to Lord Hertford early in 1815 that

> The Donegalls are in statu quo, that is very much embarrassed in their circumstances, and staving off difficulties without taking always the best means of overcoming them. Colonel O'Kelly laid an attachment upon all their goods at Ormeau. The law was tried to remove it, which, failing of effect, they are obliged to raise money upon the tenantry in the speediest manner possible. The agent Edward May, is losing his health, and is going to try the dry climate of France for his recovery. He has resisted the journey till longer delay became perilous, in the apprehension, I believe, of losing his influence with his brother-in-law. Mr and Mrs Verner [Lady Donegall's sister and brother-in-law] travel also, not for health, but economy… Lady Donegall would gladly join the travelling party but his lordship will not hear of it, though indeed it requires a singular frame of mind to be pleased with his residence here, and he will probably not stir till he feels the electrical effect of more executions.[101]

No doubt it was this kind of pressure that obliged Donegall in 1816 to agree to pay £9,000 towards O'Kelly's remaining demands on the dilapidation account for the house at Epsom – the dilapidated state of those premises must have been extreme indeed – and towards a claim concerning an annuity once granted by Donegall to a third party, in which O'Kelly had acted as security. It was in pursuit of this agreement that O'Kelly got the sheriff of County Down in 1817 to seize the contents of Ormeau and, holding the threat of a sale over Donegall's head, increased his demands still further.

Among the Grattan papers there is a revealing letter to O'Kelly from one of his relatives, probably an uncle, advising him on how to proceed so as to get the maximum advantage from the strong position he now held:

> You have now some months before the next law term – during the recess you will have repeated opportunities of protecting the marquis's property – and insure him the advantages of your forbearance – as well from your own lenity as the facility it would afford him of negotiating with advantage, and upon his own terms, with any new execution – and retard the desire in many to proceed to these extremities, when they find that the ground is so extensively occupied by you as to leave them no prospect of obtaining a guinea under the most prosperous sale of his effects. All these advantages will be greatly lessened by November, when you would be pressed to take advantage of your execution – or, decline it. You would after that period expose yourself to the assaults of his creditors, and perhaps subject yourself to all the consequences – which you have experienced several years since in many a similar situation...[102].

It is not clear whether this last remark refers to earlier attempts by other creditors to circumvent the hold that O'Kelly had established over Donegall's personal possessions; it might mean that he made his living as a moneylender and was well practised in the business of pursuing creditors. In this case, something more than financial profit might be achieved, for the writer of the letter went on:

> My own desire is, that you should turn your present advantages to the very best account. My ambition is, that you should be returned as member for Belfast...[103]

Donegall's best – perhaps his only – hope of extricating himself from his humiliations was to make an arrangement with his eldest son, who would come of age in February 1818, to break the entail (which limited what could be done with the property by the tenant-for-life) and make a new settlement. Lord Belfast's coming of age was therefore an event of crucial importance to his father, as well as being an occasion for rejoicing among the family's tenants and dependants. It was celebrated in Belfast with appropriate manifestations of public goodwill. The readers of the *Belfast News Letter* of 10 February 1818 found several columns of the paper for that day given over to an account of the illuminations of the previous Saturday. It reported:

> On Saturday evening this town was brilliantly illuminated and various fanciful devices and transparancies were exhibited by public establishments and private individuals. Similar works of rejoicing were also to be seen in the surrounding country to a great distance. Bonfires were lighted up on the neighbouring hills, and every direction manifested the glad feelings of a grateful and happy tenantry.

After a twenty-one gun salute at five o'clock, the town was soon ablaze with illuminations and the streets crowded with people to look at them. Popular among these manifestations were 'transparancies' (arrangements of transparent coloured paper on glass, lit from behind). One in front of the Academical Institution – for which Donegall had provided the ground a few years earlier and of which he was president – appropriately represented Minerva encouraging Science and rewarding Genius. The theatre in Arthur Street had a striking display of five. The polite Monsieur Gillet in Wilson's Court had one with the mottoes 'Vive le Comte de Belfast' and 'Vive le Marquis de Donegall'; while Israel Milliken, proprietor of the hot and cold baths at Peter's Hill – whose facilities, the first of their kind in the town, Donegall had made respectable by his patronage – had the front of his house 'splendidly illuminated with gas lights'. The climax of the evening came when Lady Donegall, accompanied by her children, arrived from Ormeau. 'At the end of the Long Bridge,' the *News Letter* reported, 'the carriage was stopped, the horses taken out, and her ladyship made the tour of the town, having her carriage drawn by a numerous party, everywhere greeted with those spontaneous expressions of homage and respect which indicate the most sincere regard of her ladyship and the family.'

The first step which was needed to put Lord Belfast into possession of his future rights in the property – and thus to enable him henceforth during his father's lifetime to join in any arrangements affecting its long-term interests – was the registration of a document called a deed of recovery. When this was drawn up and submitted for registration, however, O'Kelly came forward to claim that as the holder of a mortgage affecting the entire property – the mortgage given by the then Lord Belfast to Philip O'Kelly in 1794, and not hitherto regarded as of any importance – he was a necessary party to the registration. When his claim was upheld he not only refused to give his consent but even filed a bill to foreclose the mortgage. O'Kelly's hand was further strengthened by the fact – alluded to in the letter from his relative – that other creditors were also pressing Donegall very hard at the same time.

With no hope of meeting any of his obligations unless his son could speedily be put in possession of his interest in the estate, Donegall was forced to concede O'Kelly's demands in full. A new recovery deed, drawn up and signed early in 1819, acknowledged that nearly £28,000 (a good deal more than he ever claimed before) was due to O'Kelly, and made this sum a first charge on the property. O'Kelly's triumph seemed complete, or at least inevitable as soon as steps were taken to raise the money. That Donegall had no intention of paying if he could help it was not at once obvious, for as soon as the way was clear in 1819 he and his heir proceeded to sign the deed which broke the entail and thus made it possible for them to raise the money to wipe out most of the debts that had been burdening the father's income for the past twenty years. Just at this point, however, there burst a bombshell of a different sort, which not only put the intended settlement out of the question for the time being but threatened the entire future of the Donegall family and its inheritance – events which are the subject of the next chapter. Dennis O'Kelly died in 1820. His executor, a man named Harvey, took up the claim, and after him O'Kelly's son-in-law Henry Grattan, whose wife Mary had inherited her father's property.[104] Though Harvey and Grattan pursued the matter with partial success during the next two decades, they never succeeded in getting anything like £28,000 out of Donegall before he himself went to his eternal reckoning in 1844; and the claim was only settled eventually in the 1850s by the encumbered estates court.

5

HEIRS
AND DISGRACES

I T IS OBVIOUS ENOUGH WHY DONEGALL should have been anxious to break the entail and make a new settlement of the family property. Not only would he have the opportunity to extricate himself from the worst of the financial difficulties that haunted his existence, but he would also be able to make provision for the marchioness and their younger children – the kind of provision that would have been made at the time of his marriage, had he not married without his father's blessing a bride of whom his father did not approve. His heir, the earl of Belfast, had equally compelling reasons. Without any income of his own, and with little prospect of one so long as his father remained in such dire straits, he also wanted to marry. This would have made a new settlement desirable in any case. Besides, he was never very prudent or calculating about his financial affairs, if never quite his father's equal in that respect: someone described him as 'an easy-going Irishman, always in debt'.[105] So long as the father lived, the son regarded the estate as something to be milked rather than managed. He was therefore ready to agree to any arrangement, provided he got enough out of it for himself.

His intended bride was one of the daughters of the earl of Shaftesbury and the marriage was arranged to take place in the summer of 1819. Shortly before the ceremony was due, however, Shaftesbury received an anonymous letter asserting that the marriage in 1795 between the then earl of Belfast and Anna May had been illegally performed. If this were so, the children born of the union were illegitimate and the intended bridegroom had neither wealth nor title to offer his bride.

Shaftesbury of course investigated, and found that the accusation was true – or at least that there was enough doubt about the validity of the earlier ceremony to justify him in calling off the match at once.

The news created a great sensation. As Lady Charleville wrote to a friend on 13 July: 'The overthrow of Lord Belfast's marriage and fortunes, by Lord Shaftesbury having discovered that the marquis and marchioness were married under age by *licence* and not by banns, which renders it illegal and bastardizes the children irreparably, is the greatest news of the upper circles at present.' Lady Charleville's sympathy was entirely with young Chichester. 'The young lady had said she married only for money, therefore for her no pity is shown; but poor Lord Belfast to lose rank, fortune and wife at once at twenty years of age is a strong and painful catastrophe to bear properly'.[106] And indeed it must have been difficult to contemplate with equanimity such a complete reversal of expectations, particularly when the matter was so public. There must have been many letters like that of Lady Charleville. One of them, fortunately preserved, written by Lord Palmerston to his brother Sir William Temple – then minister at Naples – gives a very clear account of the affair, between an invitation to shoot grouse and news of his attendance the night before at a 'splendid but royally dull' fancy ball at Carlton House at which there had been 'little dancing and only a standing sandwich supper'. He wrote on 16 July:

> You will see in the papers a statement of a match broken off upon a discovery; it is Lord Belfast, Lord Donegall's son and one of Lord Shaftesbury's daughters. The whole thing was settled and the match was to have taken place very soon; but Shaftesbury received a letter last week to say that the marriage of Lord Donegall had not been legal and that all his children were therefore illegitimate. Upon inquiry it turned out to be perfectly true. Lady Donegall was the natural daughter of a man of the name of May, a moneylender who compelled Donegall when a youth to marry her. They were married by special licence while she was under age, and marriage by licence requires consent of legal parents, and a natural child has none to give their consent; had the marriage been by banns it would have been good. This is of course very distressing to all parties.[107]

The sixth earl of Shaftesbury, who held the title from 1811 till 1851, was the father not only of the intended bride but also of the famous philanthropist whose evangelical christianity did so much practical good for factory workers, climbing boys and lunatics. The unsympathetic author of the obituary notice in the *Annual Register* of 1851 described the late earl as 'certainly a man of undignified presence, of indistinct and hurried speech, of hasty and brusque manner…'.[108] This unfavourable opinion is borne out by what the seventh earl wrote later about his childhood, a childhood in its way as deprived of affection as those of the unfortunate children whose lot he struggled to improve: 'I and my sisters – all three of them older than myself – were brought up with great severity, moral and physical, in respect both of mind and body, the opinion of our parents being that, to render a child obedient, it should be in constant fear of its father and mother'.[109]

Perhaps, then, young Belfast had a lucky escape in 1819. He would certainly have made an odd brother-in-law for the serious-minded and painfully devout philanthropist. The ironic thing is that the marriage alliance between the families did take place, in the next generation, when his daughter (and heiress to most of the Donegall property) married Shaftesbury's heir and so united the estates. Meanwhile, the disappointed bridegroom wasted no time repining for the woman he had lost. At the end of July 1819 Lady Granville was telling her friends that Mr Chichester (he was no longer earl of Belfast) had fallen deeply in love with Lady Harriet Butler (daughter of the first earl of Glengall) and, it was thought, would propose to her very soon.

The cause of the disaster in 1819, as Palmerston explains, was a technicality of the law governing the ceremony of marriage. Before 1753, when Hardwicke's act 'for the better preventing of clandestine marriages' had been placed on the statute book, there had been very few legal conditions laid down as to what constituted a valid ceremony. If performed under a special licence (as virtually all marriages in good society were) the affair could take place privately, even secretly, since it did not have to be performed in a church, could be done at any hour of the day or night, and did not require witnesses – apart from the officiating clergyman, who could be a private chaplain or crony.[110] It had been all too common for unscrupulous rakes to kidnap or elope with young heiresses and go through a form of marriage in order to gain control of their fortunes, or for dubious women to trap young heirs into marriages which they and their families regretted. Particularly notorious were the marriages contracted within the bounds of the Fleet prison, from which one disreputable clergyman had a steady source of income. During the debates on the bill in the House of Commons it was stated as a fact that as many as 6,000 marriages had taken place in the prison chapel in one year.[111] There were so many abuses that parliament at last decided to intervene, though there was bitter opposition (by Horace Walpole, among others, who detested Hardwicke) against this restriction on liberty.

The act of 1753 certainly succeeded in its aim of making clandestine marriages of that kind difficult in England (the law in Scotland remained lax, hence the continuing popularity among eloping lovers of the journey to Gretna) by rendering invalid any ceremony not performed in a parish church before at least two witnesses and, in the case of minors, without the consent of parents or guardians. Most marriages were thereafter preceded by the public calling of the banns in church. Where a special licence was used the ceremony still had to be public and the consent of the proper parties was still needed. Unfortunately, however, the curing of one set of evils created another lot, worse because it was the innocent and well-intentioned who were most easily injured. Since the least irregularity in observing the requirements of the new law invalidated a marriage, and the good faith of the parties counted for nothing, it became easy to find grounds for nullity, with distressing consequences for any children who had been born in the meantime and with serious effects in some cases on the inheritance of property – not to mention the grievance created for members of nonconforming sects who now had to marry in the parish church. Things were made particularly difficult for illegitimate children who wished to marry as minors, for in the eye of the law they had no parents who could either give consent or appoint guardians who could give consent; such children were obliged to go to the court of chancery for the appointment of guardians. It became notorious that numbers of people whose marriages had been celebrated in good faith were caught by the technicalities of the law, with the result that their children were made illegitimate and unable to inherit property that was entailed. This is what happened to the earl of Belfast and his brothers in 1819. Donegall's rights for his own lifetime were not affected, but after his death the entire property would pass – unless he married again and had a son – to his nephew Arthur, son of his recently deceased brother Spencer Chichester. By all accounts this young man behaved extremely well towards his uncle and cousins in this unlooked-for change in his prospects. Palmerston remarked that he had 'behaved like an angel and offered to make any arrangement that could be proposed on his part' (in fact he proposed that £100,000 should be raised on the security of the estates to support Donegall's children, including a guaranteed income of nearly £3,000 a year for the eldest)[112] while Lady Charleville wrote, 'I hear Mr Chichester (rightful heir) behaves well, but he cannot prevent the entail affecting his heirs nor the title descending to him from his cousin.'[113]

It was a legal technicality that rendered the Donegall marriage invalid after nearly twenty-five years and the birth of seven children. Anna May was the illegitimate child of her father, so that his consent to the marriage was not sufficient; and no legal guardian had been appointed who could have given proper consent (and no doubt would have done so, since there was no question of her being an heiress whose property might be lost by fraud). Furthermore, despite all that was later claimed, there seems to have been no genuine doubt about her being under age. The entry in the marriage register reads:

> The right honourable George Augustus Chichester of this parish, but commonly called Earl of Belfast, and Anna May of the same parish, spinster, a minor, were married in this church by license and with consent of Edward May, esq., father of the said minor, this eighth day of August, one thousand seven hundred and ninety five. J. Thomas.
> This marriage was solemnized between us
>   Belfast   Anna May
> In the presence of
>   Edward May: Eliza Lind: Eliza May.[114]

What was evidently concealed, in order to make the ceremony appear valid and binding, was the illegitimacy which made the father's consent insufficient. The ceremony in Marylebone parish church had not been exactly the kind that the law of 1753 had been intended to prevent, for its victim – if there was a victim – had been not the heiress of twenty but the heir of twenty-six. Nevertheless it had been a clandestine affair, carried through with a good deal of haste and secrecy and bearing out Palmerston's story that May had obliged the foolish Lord Belfast to marry his daughter as a way of getting out of the debtors' prison. It is significant that only the girl's relations were present at the wedding and acted as witnesses (Eliza Lind, of whom there is no other mention anywhere, may have been her real mother). The Mays seem to have made sure that young Belfast had no time for second thoughts, and no chance of healing the breach with his father, who would certainly have opposed the match and would have done his best to stop it. The very fact that the wedding took place where it did is also significant, for Marylebone was much used as a parish of convenience by outsiders who for one reason or another did not wish to use their own. In the last three months of 1817 the banns of 284 couples were published in Marylebone; of these 568 people all but two were said to be residents of the parish, whereas the great majority were in fact non-residents.[115] If not exactly a 'Fleet marriage', then, the 1795 ceremony had been the next best thing to one. However, since even to Mrs McTier's sharply critical eye Anna was an attractive and lively young woman, the victim had probably been willing enough – and indeed had done better for himself in the way of a wife than he deserved, if it had not been for her rapacious relatives.

Though Belfast and its neighbourhood must have been thunderstruck by the news that its resident landlord and his wife were not in the eyes of the law man and wife, and that the young man whose coming of age had been celebrated just a year before was no longer the rightful heir to the Chichester estates, there was an astonishing reticence in the local press about the matter. It is hard to imagine in the circumstances anything more discreet than this note in the *Belfast News Letter* three months afterwards:

> We rejoice to hear that the late unpleasant rumours affecting the interests of a noble family will, in all probability, be speedily set to rest in the most satisfactory manner. Very eminent counsel having been consulted, we understand that their opinions are decidedly favourable on the point in question.[116]

We know from other sources that the news spread very quickly, so quickly that everyone in local society knew it before Lady Donegall herself did. A local resident named Harvey (port surveyor of Belfast) wrote to Lord Hertford describing an extraordinary scene at a party attended by the marchioness:

> Your lordship can hardly imagine the sensation which this unexpected embarrassment of the Donegall family has produced in this quarter, nor how much it was heightened by what occurred at a private party which was given in this neighbourhood at the very moment the first intimation of this disaster had become the universal subject of everyone's thoughts and conversation – when, to the surprise, more than surprise, of everyone, Lady Donegall made her appearance and arrived rather late, as if to encounter the astonished looks of the whole company.

BELFAST ROYAL HOTEL,

DONEGALL-PLACE,

(*Opposite the Linen-Hall*)

N.B. All Mail and Day Coaches, entering, or leaving Belfast, pass by the Door.

The Royal Hotel, Belfast, *c*.1830. Formerly the town residence of the Donegalls, the house had been converted into a hotel in 1824 by their ex-butler Kerns.

Scarcely was anyone able to address her. All conversation ceased, and way was silently made for her to the upper end of the room, where with some embarrassment the lady of the house paid her some attention, which she received with much ease, displaying great spirits, and appearing in fact the only unconcerned person in the room; which, I believe, was literally the case, for what appears almost incredible, she was the only person uninformed of what had happened, and her subsequent conduct since the news has reached her, sufficiently evinces that it did not proceed from the wish of acting a part, or from want of feeling. It produced, however, a scene which Mrs Harvey, who was present, and could hardly answer her ladyship's civil questions, described to me as very striking.[117]

The only references in the local press, apart from the one already quoted, were occasional notices of the progress of the legal moves by which the family sought to establish the legitimacy of the marriage. Harvey's letter to Lord Hertford explained the background to the *Belfast News Letter's* talk of counsel's opinions:

The shape which I understand the question will now assume, will be a bill filed in chancery for the ostensible object of closing a mortgage with a view of settling a part of the estate which, as it can only be done by Lord Belfast's concurrence, and as his concurrence can be valid only in the supposition of no informality in the marriage of Lady Donegall, will open that interesting investigation upon which his lordship's rank and estate, and perhaps eventually the undisturbed residence of his family in these counties may ultimately depend.[118]

The family may have put a bold face on it, but the issue of the chancery case was thought to be very uncertain, despite the favourable opinions of some leading lawyers; for as Harvey said, 'Not only unprofessional people are divided, but the lawyers entertain equally opposite opinions.' He also mentions that if the earl of Belfast failed in his suit there was a plan to put the second son, Edward, in his place, 'grounding his claim to legitimacy upon the circumstance of his father and mother having resided in Scotland, as man and wife, previous to his birth...' The lord advocate was said to have a favourable opinion on this claim, but again others thought differently. The third possibility was said to be an act of parliament, but Harvey could not see how this would help, since changes in the law were not normally retrospective.[119] The chancery case proceeded with the exquisite delay inevitable in that court. No quick result could be expected, and the result when it came might be unfavourable. So another case was begun in May 1821, this time in the consistory court, the ecclesiastical court which at that time dealt with all divorce proceedings. Ostensibly a suit to declare the marriage null and void, its real object was to establish the validity of the ceremony beyond doubt. The main evidence was supplied by old Lady May and her daughter Mrs Verner, who had both been present at the marriage, and the marchioness's old nurse Mary Mundy, who had remained with her former charge and, now aged eighty-three, still lived with the family at Ormeau. Mrs Mundy's deposition, signed with her mark, is a poignant document beneath its formal legal language – and suspiciously exact on the vital point of Anna May's date of birth, which was said to be 10 March 1774, which would have made her of age by six months at the time of her wedding in August 1795. Mundy said she had been first engaged to take over Anna from the wet nurse in the summer of that year, when the infant appeared to be about three months old. When Anna was about a year old her nurse went to Hampshire to live and took the child with her, because she had a friend living in Hampshire 'where there was plenty of milk and butter and good air and where she knew she would be welcome'. When Anna was just over three years of age she was brought by her nurse to London, to Holles Street where the Mays then lived. Mundy says that she delivered the child into the care of Edward May and his wife, whom she describes as Anna's 'father and mother'.[120] The phrase perhaps indicates that Lady May had been her husband's mistress before she became his wife. If she was not Anna's real mother she was certainly an accommodating wife, for the child was brought up thereafter as her own.

The evidence of Mrs Verner reveals that at the time of the marriage in 1795 there had been some debate in her own family as to the bride's age and the legality of the ceremony. Mrs Verner said she remembered being present in her parents' house, she could not be certain of the exact date, when the banns were published for a second marriage between the earl of Belfast and her sister, about two months after the first. She recalled a discussion between her mother and a clergyman named Laurence 'relative to the supposed invalidity of the marriage between the said marquis and marchioness of Donegall and to the necessity of another marriage being solemnized between them'. Lady May had told the clergyman, when he asked why the banns had been published for a second marriage, that her husband had thought – mistakenly – that Anna had not been of age at the time of the first ceremony. She said she would not have a second marriage, since it was quite unnecessary. The outcome was that no second ceremony took place. Mrs Verner said she recalled the incident so vividly because she had been present in the church of St Mary le Bone at the wedding such a short time before.[121] The likeliest interpretation of this tale is that Edward May had indeed persuaded the weak (and perhaps also infatuated) Lord Belfast to marry in haste a daughter whom he knew to be both under age and illegitimate, but that when he tried later to make everything safe by removing the illegality his wife would not allow him to proceed, perhaps because it would have drawn attention to the girl's illegitimacy.

Neither the case in chancery nor the one in the divorce court reached its conclusion. It was eventually a change in the law that saved the day for the Donegalls and allowed Lord Belfast to become the legitimate heir again and able to join with his father after all in settling the family's affairs. It had long been admitted that the act of 1753 had produced injustices because its strict technicalities left no scope for the good faith of the parties, however amply demonstrated. The Donegall affair was only the latest of these injustices, and attracted particular notice only because the people concerned were socially prominent, the property affected one of the largest in the country and the discovery of the illegality so public and dramatic. The immediate need of the Donegalls and others in the same embarrassing plight was met by an amendment to the 1753 act, passed in the summer of 1822, which validated 'all cases of marriage had and solemnized by licence before the passing of this act... where the parties shall have continued to live together as husband and wife till the death of one of them, or till the passing of this act...'[122]

The bill which brought about this salvation was proposed in the House of Commons on 27 March 1822 by Dr Phillimore, who since 1817 had made three earlier attempts to alter the law, all of them successful in the lower House but thrown out by the Lords. In the course of a long and powerful speech he reviewed the iniquitous results of the 1753 act, dwelling in particular on the scandalous ease with which marriages could be annulled long after they had taken place (after thirty-eight years in one recent case) and on the harsh lot of illegitimate children whose marriages – made in good faith – had been declared invalid because they were found to have lacked proper consent. Over forty such cases had come before the divorce courts of the province of Canterbury since 1810. As regius professor of civil law at Oxford (a post he held for forty-six years) and an expert in ecclesiastical cases, Phillimore was an impressive advocate. His proposals included a clause making the benefit of the bill retrospective where both parties to a marriage were over twenty-one and had continued to live together as man and wife. He was fortunately able to refer to a couple of precedents for doing this – both concerning minor amendments to the marriage law – where the retrospective principle had been accepted without difficulty.[123]

It was not accepted without difficulty on this occasion. In the House of Lords the venerable lord chancellor, Eldon, spoke strongly against it (fifty years before, as a young man, he had eloped to Scotland with an heiress). The supporters of the measure in the upper House, however, not only accepted that it should be retrospective but extended its operation to all marriages contracted since 1753. This went much farther than Phillimore had proposed, and raised the awkward question of the rights of people who had acquired property through the misfortunes of relatives debarred from inheriting by the working of the 1753 act. Several peers – Shaftesbury was one of them, not surprisingly – lodged strong protests against the final form of the bill. The aged chancellor, to whose lawyer's mind the retrospective principle was completely unacceptable, is reported as having said: 'I consider it neither more nor less than a legal robbery: so help me God. I have but a short time to remain with you, but I trust it will be hereafter known that I used every means in my power to prevent its passing into a law.'[124] The duke of Richmond had earlier presented a petition from Arthur Chichester, the heir presumptive to the Donegall property, complaining of the retrospective effect of the bill and praying that it might not pass into law and thus deprive him of his rights. His plea had some effect, for Lord Liverpool (the prime minister) tried to bring in a clause to prevent the measure from extending to any cases already in the courts – which would have excluded Donegall – but most of the peers rejected this. A similar petition presented to the Commons at the second reading of the bill also failed. Chichester's final effort, a petition to the king, had no better success, royal assent to the bill being given on 22 July.[125] There was evidently a good deal of sympathy for Donegall, especially among his fellow peers; it seems clear that this bill succeeded in the upper House, where previous ones had failed, largely because of the Donegall case.

The opponents of the bill in the Commons certainly thought so and said so. One remarked that 'It was notorious to every man, both in and out of that House, that the present measure was not founded upon general principles of legislation, but had been introduced for the express purpose of meeting an individual case'.[126] When Phillimore denied this, the attorney general remarked that 'it was impossible not to perceive that there were persons who looked forward to the bill with interested motives'.[127] Another opponent said he 'had heard a noble lady had had a great hand in framing this bill...' and also remarked that only twenty lines of the original bill were left, 'while ten pages of new and undigested matter was added by their lordships'.[128] In the final debate in the Commons, on 12 July, Phillimore and his friends easily won the day, however, by 122 votes to 20. The amendments made by the Lords, he said, had been adopted

> after the most deliberate consideration that in our days had been applied to any bill which had been sent from this House to the other branch of legislature. Within the last five years three bills had been sent to the House of Lords on this subject, varying in form from each other, but agreeing in substance. All these were rejected; but on the

present occasion the House of Lords had not only adopted this the fourth bill but... had carried the principle of reform infinitely farther than the House of Commons had contemplated.[129]

However badly the amendments might be drafted, he argued, the important thing was to have a reform that the Lords would at long last accept, rather than lose the bill altogether by haggling about its imperfections.

One of the most distinguished supporters of the bill at all its stages in the House of Commons was the foreign secretary, Robert Stewart, usually known to history as Viscount Castlereagh but now marquis of Londonderry and – as an Irish peer – a member of the lower House. He was much in favour of the retrospective principle and 'could see no reason whatsoever for withholding the operation of the present measure from those who had already gone into the ecclesiastical courts'. Though, like Phillimore, he denied supporting it because it had been introduced to meet a particular case, he thought 'it ought to be no objection to the bill if there was a case of such manifest oppression from the existing law, as forced an attention to the law, and the necessity of its amendment upon the consideration of the House'.[130] As an Ulster landowner himself, with large estates near Belfast, he was obviously referring to the case of his neighbour Donegall. Incidentally this must have been one of Castlereagh's last speeches, for exactly a month later, worn out by overwork and worry about his health, he cut his throat. His successor as foreign secretary, Canning, also spoke in support of the bill, though he prophesied correctly that a new measure would soon be needed to amend and explain it. In the year 1823 a much more sweeping general reform of the marriage law was carried, which repealed both the 1753 act and its 1822 amendment. The marriage act of 1823, though subsequently altered and modified, remained the basis of the law, so far as marriages in England were concerned, until 1949. On the particular point which had made the Donegall marriage invalid it laid down that, in the case of children who were under age, the father or the guardians or – if illegitimate – the mother were the proper people to give consent. Only marriages which had been knowingly and wilfully performed elsewhere than in a church, or without the banns having been called (or a licence got), or by someone not in holy orders were in future to be void.[131]

The three years from July 1819, when the thunderbolt had fallen, to July 1822, when the amendment of the law at last legitimised his marriage and his seven children, must have been anxious ones for Donegall, not least because it must have been even more difficult than before for him to borrow money. He had spent much of the time in London, at any rate while the courts were sitting. Lord Hertford's correspondent Harvey reported in October 1819 that the distracted peer was then in London 'collecting legal assistance, and waiting for money which may enable him to return...'; and we learn from an incidental reference in the local press that he returned to Belfast in September 1821 after a long absence.[132] The happy outcome of the affair prompted the editor of the *Belfast News Letter*, for long a model of restraint, to write on 26 July 1822, just four days after the amendment became law: 'From the day the charter was first obtained for Belfast by the distinguished ancestor of Lord Donegall's family, no event has occurred that excited so many happy sensations as the intimation of the passing of the act.' Local rejoicing included a congratulatory dinner attended by 240 people, at which no fewer than forty-one toasts were drunk and the company expressed its joy at the happy outcome – presumably with increasing incoherence as the evening went on.

$$6$$

THE
PRODIGAL FATHER

T HE NEW SETTLEMENT of the Donegall property was signed on 28 October 1822.[133] Such documents, couched in repetitive legal jargon, are not so interesting to read as family letters; but since this settlement was to have a profound effect both upon the future of the family and upon the history of Belfast it is worth a careful look. In order to clear off most of Donegall's personal debts and leave no more than £45,000 as a permanent burden on the estate, £217,000 was to be raised. Of this sum, Lord Belfast was to have £25,000 and a further £12,000 within three years for his own use, and his father £10,000. The son was also to have the right to borrow on his expectations up to a limit of £100,000, but none of this was to be raised out of the estate so long as his father was alive. The opportunity was also taken to provide a jointure of £3,000 for the marchioness if she should outlive her husband, and 'portions' totalling £70,000 for their younger children. The entail was then re-established, with a life interest to the father and succession to the eldest son and his heirs. Lord Belfast, having kept his bride Harriet Butler waiting for three anxious years while the marriage case was in doubt, hastened to marry her. 'Bel and the Dragon' someone called them, because he was so handsome and she so hot-tempered.

£217,000 was a very large sum of money, equivalent to several millions in modern currency. Normally it would have been raised by selling off part of the property. In Donegall's case, however, the bids might have been affected by awkward doubts in the minds of would-be purchasers as to whether they would get a clear title and might not find themselves sucked into one of those complicated lawsuits in which he was known to be continually involved. Such considerations frequently hampered sales of Irish land. In any case, land was not fetching a good price in the 1820s: the agricultural depression that followed the end of the war against France made buyers hard to find and prices low. Possibly, too, Donegall craftily intended to keep his creditors in the dark as much as possible about the amount of money actually raised – the way things turned out certainly makes one suspect this. A sale, even by private treaty, as most sales of land in Ireland were, would have given a shrewd observer some idea of the purchase price.

Whatever the reasons, it was decided to raise the money not by selling land but by granting perpetual leases – leases for the lives of three named people, with a covenant allowing the tenant to put in new lives as the existing ones died off, on payment of a modest sum, for as long as he wished. 'Eternity in parchment' was how another Ulster landowner described such grants. The rents to be paid were very moderate (they had in most cases been fixed half a century earlier) but lump sums in cash were also demanded. Once he had given his money and got his lease the tenant was secure, so long as he paid his rent and kept a careful eye on the obituary notices for news of his 'lives'. He could do as he liked with the property – sell it, mortgage it, sublet it, build on it – subject only to such things as mineral and water rights, which the landlord retained.

Leases for the lives of named persons (usually three) were the commonest form of long lease in the eighteenth century. They often had a term of years as well – thirty-one or sometimes forty-one – so that the tenant was guaranteed at least that length of time and with luck might do rather better. In fact the average duration of the three-life lease was over fifty years, and some ran for much longer; the many tenants who had George III's name put in their leases when he was still a boy got a particularly good run for their money, since he lived to be eighty-two. The idea that the length of a lease should depend on a gamble of this kind seems very strange to our way of thinking. Like so much else in the past that seems at first sight merely quaint, it had a thoroughly practical and hard-headed explanation. In Ireland before 1829 the voters in county elections consisted of those who either owned land outright or had a life interest in it. Landowners who wanted to increase their political influence in county elections made their tenants into 'freeholders' by giving them leases which contained at least one life in the term and, for safety's sake, usually three.

Leases for lives renewable for ever were in a different category, since the landowner was in no position to influence his tenant's vote by threatening not to renew the lease. These perpetuities were largely peculiar to Ireland. The commission which under the chairmanship of the earl of Devon looked into the question of Irish land in the 1840s referred to the perpetual lease as 'a species of tenure, scarcely known elsewhere, which prevails very extensively in that country, one-seventh of Ireland being said to be held under it'.[134] Some estates had a large part of their acreage let to perpetual leaseholders, usually people of some wealth and substance who in turn sublet most of their property to the farmers who actually occupied the land – so in that respect there was nothing odd about Donegall's move. The odd thing about it was the date. By the nineteenth century new perpetuities were rare, for the very good reason that they and the middlemen who held them were no longer regarded as desirable by most landlords. In earlier days during times of political uncertainty, or in areas where it had been difficult to collect rents from the occupiers, landowners had sometimes been glad to settle for a steady if fixed income by giving long leases to middlemen. By the end of the eighteenth century, with agricultural prices and rents increasing, the whole trend was the other way, towards shorter leases which would allow a landowner to raise his rents more frequently. Granting large numbers of perpetuities at such a late date was therefore a clear sign of financial desperation on the part of the Donegall family. During the previous century none had been granted, not even in County Donegal where most of the tenants were big middlemen.

By the terms of the settlement the money raised by fines was to be paid to trustees, the chief of whom was Edward May's successor as vicar of Belfast (May had died in 1819 at Pisa), the Reverend Arthur Chichester Macartney. Macartney's brother Joseph, a lawyer, negotiated the 'sales' and drew up the leases. It was a large operation. During the next ten years well over 1,500 leases were granted, 600 of them for property in and about the town of Belfast, most of the rest for land in County Antrim. Nearly all the ground of Belfast, 70,000 acres in Antrim and nearly 77,000 acres in Donegal were affected – in fact the greater part of the estate. One reason why so much land had to be disposed of was that for some years Donegall had been raising money from the tenants by giving or renewing leases for sixty-one years at the existing rents, in return for cash. The longer his existing lease, the less a tenant was prepared to pay for a perpetuity. A good deal of negotiation went on, with tenants trying to get the best bargain they could and Joseph Macartney trying to raise as much money as possible for his employer. There are hints in the estate papers that he also made money for himself in the process. He was certainly in a position to do so, by giving preference to bidders who would buy his favour. Rumours of this were rife at the time. A great neighbouring proprietor, Lord Downshire – not a man given to idle gossip about his fellow landowners – told his agent that the Upton family nearly lost the perpetuity of its 7,000-acre leasehold estate in County Antrim to a rival bidder (a man who had made a fortune in the linen trade) and had had to pay Macartney £500 to make sure of it.[135]

The leases were an attractive bargain to anyone with money or the means to borrow it, as the number of takers suggests. The leading merchants in and about Belfast – all the big names in the linen trade, for example – bought perpetuities of their business premises and their homes. In addition, several of them invested on a large scale and so became landlords of parts of the town. By far the biggest investor of this sort was William Tennent, a banker, who took twenty separate leases. The Ashmore family took ten, the Browns eight. Cunningham Greg, a very substantial man, took fourteen and in addition country holdings of more than 2,000 acres. In County Donegal all the big middlemen – such as the Youngs of Culdaff with well over 7,000 acres, the Harts of Kilderry (nearly 5,000), Sir Robert Ferguson (over 6,500) and Sir Arthur Chichester (5,500) – hastened to make their estates permanent. A few very small farmers in Donegal also managed to buy; one paid £30 for his farm of eight acres with its annual rent of less than £2.

In County Antrim, where small tenants were numerous and comparatively prosperous, many saved or borrowed the money for this unique opportunity of acquiring their own land. In the 1830s, when the first ordnance survey was being carried out, the compiler of the field report for the parish of Donegore wrote:

> A recent source of benefit to the farmers of this parish was the embarrassed circumstances of their landlord, the marquis of Donegall who to enable him to raise money, was obliged to grant leases in perpetuity at an almost nominal rent. This had for some time been foreseen, and many of the tenants in this parish by their frugality and industry were enabled to take advantage of the opportunity by paying the necessary purchase.[136]

The writer made the same remark about the neighbouring parish of Kilbride. From the tenants' point of view, a landlord who would do almost anything to get his hands on ready money was a godsend.

The earliest of the leases were handwritten on parchment, as all such documents used to be, but this method must have been both too slow and too expensive for the large number needed, and the parchments were soon replaced by printed forms. The wording of the leases was simply copied from the long leases of the past, except of course for the new covenant for perpetual renewal. The lives which were put into all the leases were those of three of Donegall's sons. Apart from the usual details about rent and what rights the landlord was to retain (minerals, game, water and so on), each lease stated that the lump sum agreed was to be paid to the Reverend A.C. Macartney, to be applied by him towards the purposes described in the deed of settlement. Though the capital value of the property would thus be reduced considerably, at least Donegall would no longer be burdened with the debts that reduced his income and harassed his existence, while his son would be free of both the debts and the lawsuits arising from them. Curiously enough, but not surprisingly, that was not the way things worked out, for when Donegall died in 1844 it was revealed that the debts supposed to have been paid off in the 1820s were still owing. Somehow the father had managed to squander the money, and to conceal the fact from his son.

How he did so is a mystery. There is a clue, however, in the following passage from Benn: 'Between 1822 and 1831 new leases, renewable for ever, were very extensively made by the late marquis, at the old rents, and in consideration of fines professed to be paid to the trustees.'[137] Benn, who was a young man at the time of all this excitement among the tenants of the estate (the first version of his book was published in 1823), was always benevolent in his references to Donegall, whom he regarded as good-natured but weak. What he clearly implies in his comment about the leases, however, is that the money said to have been paid to the trustees was really paid to Donegall himself, who thus for the first time in many years had large amounts of cash to spend as he liked. Whether or not it had been his intention all along to raise money in a way that would enable him to baulk his creditors yet again is impossible to discover. Nor do we know if Lord Belfast connived at his father's actions. Perhaps he neither knew nor cared so long as his own demands were met. When he succeeded his father he certainly

expressed dismay and astonishment to find the estate still heavily encumbered with debts that were supposed to have been paid twenty
years before; and it is hard to believe he could have remained indifferent, had he known of what amounted to a really gigantic fraud at his
expense. For, as Benn points out, he had shown a remarkable disregard
for his own personal interests by agreeing to the settlement. Perhaps
the best guess is that he was pretty careless and his father pretty crafty.
As so often with Donegall, life echoed fiction. In *The Absentee*, Maria
Edgeworth writes of the debt-ridden Irish peer Lord Clonbrony: 'He
could not bring himself positively to deny that he had debts and difficulties; but he would by no means open the state of his affairs to his
son: "No father is called upon to do that", said he to himself; "none but
a fool would do it"'. Foolish though he was in many ways, Donegall
was not so foolish as that.

However he accomplished it, Donegall in effect contrived over a
period of ten years to supplement his already substantial, if rather de-
pleted, income by sums in cash equivalent to several millions in modern money. Exactly how he spent it all is an insoluble mystery in the
absence of proper accounts. He could afford, among other things, to
indulge on a more lavish scale his enthusiasm for hunting. Fisherwick
Lodge, his house at Doagh in County Antrim, was substantially altered
and enlarged at some point in the early nineteenth century, with extensive stabling, kennels for hounds and improvements to the grounds
(including the construction of an artificial lake). Some of these changes
may have been made in the 1820s, when the Doagh Hunt evidently
flourished as never before and Donegall entertained its supporters with
a hospitality which prompted William Percy in 1826 to perpetrate his
'Panegyric Stanzas', of which the following is a sufficient example:

> See Doagh throng'd with grandeur, see Farrell's great Inn,
> Where our fine Antrim Hunters festivity win;
> Where a pattern's afforded, admired by all,
> Of the generous landlord in great Donegall.
> Hark away! hark away! whilst we fervently pray,
> That our kindest of landlords may still bear the sway.

During these years Donegall also had a yacht, the *Zoe*, which he frequently raced – and no doubt backed with heavy wagers – at local
regattas.

The only accounts that have survived – lists of monies totalling

£86,000 paid on Donegall's behalf by Joseph Macartney between March 1823 and May 1826[138] – show that one major item of expenditure was the rebuilding and refurnishing of the house at Ormeau. Though probably extended to accommodate the family and its servants, Ormeau Cottage was always a very modest place for someone of Donegall's rank and position. When the marquis of Londonderry was visited at Mount Stewart in 1818 by a Russian grand duke (who had met his son Castlereagh at the Congress of Vienna) and invited the Donegalls to dinner, he was horrified when Donegall then failed to offer hospitality to the distinguished guest, but reflected that the owner of Ormeau had 'neither a house, establishment nor the proper means to entertain the royal duke as was fitting the landlord of so respectable a property and important a trading town'.[139] In 1823 work began on the larger and much more imposing residence known as Ormeau House, designed by the young Irish architect William Vitruvius Morrison. Morrison had begun his career by assisting his more famous father Richard (later Sir Richard) Morrison to build or alter some notable Irish houses. He himself claimed to have introduced the Tudor revival style into Ireland, after a trip to England in 1821 during which he made a particular study of Tudor buildings. Ormeau House was probably the first of his

Ormeau House in 1832, from the drawing by Joseph Molloy
in *Belfast Scenery in Thirty Views.*

Irish commissions in this style, followed shortly by the reconstruction of Glenarm Castle. The building depicted by Joseph Molloy in 1832 and by W.H. Burgess in 1841 does indeed look like a Tudor manor house with its mullioned windows, turrets, buttresses and numerous chimneys.[140]

Though Morrison drew the designs (a few of which survive), their execution was directed by humbler local architects and carried out by local workmen. Macartney's accounts show that almost everything in the way of materials and labour for the building was supplied by Belfast merchants and tradesmen – to the value of £7,000 or more during those years alone. The new house, which incorporated the old one, was very large: the ground area, including attached offices, was over 20,000 square feet and the floor area twice that. Morrison's additions included such Tudor features as a banqueting hall and a long gallery, as well as a new entrance hall with an impressive wagon roof; upstairs there were at least a dozen principal bedrooms. Such a place, permanently occupied, provided employment for a large number of staff and servants and valuable custom for a great many shopkeepers and suppliers, as Macartney's accounts show. There was, for example, very heavy expenditure on horses: an average of £1,600 a year was paid out to one provision merchant for forage alone.

After ten years of raising money by fines, the sales of leases abruptly ceased. By that time about £24,000 – well over two-thirds of the annual rental – had been let in perpetuity. Among other things this meant that the greater part of the income from the property could never be increased. Exactly how much money was raised in fines is not known, but it must have been a very large sum. From the leases that have survived we know what was paid in about 600 cases, and on average these tenants paid fourteen times the annual rent. Fourteen times £24,000 is over £330,000. If this figure is anywhere near the mark, we must believe not only that the money raised was not used as intended, but also that far more than the £217,000 mentioned in the settlement was taken out of the value of the estate. The reason why the sales stopped, according to Lord Downshire, was that Lord Belfast would consent to no more because he was dissatisfied with his share. As Downshire explained to his chief agent Reilly in 1833:

Lord Belfast has agreed to the leases for ever, so long as his father answered his calls for money, and Mr McCartney negotiated his bills in

Belfast. When those two sources were parched up, Lord Belfast refused his assent to more renewals, and this resistance on his part produced an equitable adjustment to the extent of raising in the way of mortgage or some other way, 80 or £90,000 of which McCartney obtained £25,000 and Wallace [another Belfast attorney] about £20,000, and Lord Belfast was to have £2,000 a year additional and £3,000 ditto to pay the interest of other debts which he contracted long ago.[141]

As Downshire also remarked, 'all this arrangement however is only temporary, and the family will require a very large sum out of the dilapidated estate before long to meet their many heavy demands'. This was only too true. By 1836 Donegall's financial circumstances were as bad as they had ever been, so bad that he could not even continue his subscription to local charities because control of his money was in hands other than his own. When a deputation of worried trustees proposed to call on him he put them off with the following explanation to one of its members:

> Colonel Coulson informed me of the intention of yourself and some other gentlemen to call on me as a deputation from the fever hospital and other charitable institutions in Belfast, to which I was a subscriber, for the purpose of getting my sanction in writing to an application to the lord chancellor that my subscription should be paid out of the funds in the hands of the receiver. I hope it is perfectly known to the inhabitants of Belfast and to the gentlemen who compose the committees of those excellent institutions, how much I value their usefulness and how deeply I deplore my inability to continue my subscription and the difficulty I am placed in by being obliged to decline the requests, for I feel that whilst my embarrassments continue and that I am unable to discharge just debts which I owe I would not be authorised in being a party to sanction an application as is desired.[142]

In view of what we know about Donegall's record as a discharger of debts his pious remarks about getting his priorities right are amusing; such was his reputation for evading payment that he appeared in print in a satirical tale of the period as 'the Marquis of Done-'em-all'.[143] The truth was that recent changes in the law concerning enforcement of debts in Ireland had given some of his creditors greater power than ever before to have receivers appointed by the courts. To ensure that interest was paid regularly by the creditor, his rents were collected by the receiver and lodged in a fund controlled by the court. A few years later, in 1840, these powers were extended still further. During the last years of his life, then, Donegall found himself increasingly hampered by receivers and became little more than a remittance man.

This curious outcome of an operation that had been intended to clear the estate of debt was bad enough. Worse still was the effect on the family's power and influence. We shall be looking in more detail at the decline in its political power. Even in a practical and immediate way, the sale of so many perpetuities had inevitable effects. Whereas before 1822 Donegall really had been the owner of the whole of Belfast and district, he was now only the ground landlord. The tenants were their own masters and could do as they liked without having to get the approval – or fear the disapproval – of the estate office, so long as they paid their rents and renewed the lives in their leases. The difference was particularly noticeable in the matter of new building. During the period 1825–45 Belfast grew considerably and many new streets were laid out. But whereas Georgian Belfast had been planned and controlled by Donegall's father, through the kind of leases that were given, and the expansion of the town influenced since 1799 by himself through grants of land and building leases, he had scarcely any part in the later developments. It used to be thought that Belfast's unprecedented growth in the latter half of the century was made possible by the sale of the ground by the third marquis in the encumbered estates court in the 1850s. In fact it could have taken place at any time from 1830 onwards, when the landlord lost control. Though the way was thus left open for the enterprise of its citizens – and Donegall himself was not the man to meet the need – Belfast in its period of greatest growth might have benefited from the direction of an owner with enlightened ideas about planning and architecture. Its only public park until the end of the century was the demesne at Ormeau, one of the few areas remaining to the family, which was leased to the corporation in 1869 by the third marquis.

The change in Donegall's relations with the citizens of Belfast is best illustrated by the story of the water commissioners and their attempts to improve the supply to the town during the 1830s.[144] The history of the water supply was a peculiar one. The Charitable Institution or Poorhouse had been built in 1771. In 1795 the Charitable Society had got a lease of certain springs and watercourses from the first marquis and from then until 1840 was responsible for supplying the needs of the town, a task which was deputed to water commissioners who paid a rent of £750 to the society. The growth of the town soon made the supply inadequate, and by 1803 the society – of which he himself was president – was petitioning Donegall for more springs. This approach was favourably received, though there was at first some difficulty in arranging a meeting, as the following note from Donegall reveals:

> I am extremely sorry that I was not at home on Thursday last accord-
> ing to my appointment, but Wednesday which was my hunting day
> proving so bad it was postponed till Thursday of which I have to re-
> proach myself of not having given you due information and for which
> I beg a thousand pardons.[145]

New leases were given, and some years later the ground for a new reservoir was also granted. In the 1820s Donegall intervened successfully on behalf of the society in a dispute with a government department, which moved the committee to pass a motion of thanks to him '…for the frequent paternal and important services he had rendered to this institution and particularly for his late successful application to the lords commissioners of his majesty's treasury…' As the historian of the Charitable Society says: 'It is impossible to read the involved story of the water supply without being aware of his many acts of kindness and generosity or of the esteem and the affection in which he was held'.[146]

That happy state of affairs was altered in the following decade, when the water supply was again in a critical state. By that time Donegall and his son had leased to various manufacturers, in perpetuity, all the water not already let to the society. This did not prevent them from threatening to obtain an act of parliament to supply the town themselves, as a way of obstructing the commissioners' proposals, in order to force up the amount that would be offered to buy out any remaining rights the family might have in the ownership of the precious resource.

As Donegall wrote in 1837:

> …I think it right to state I shall oppose any… bill no matter by whom
> introduced, unless a satisfactory arrangement be previously made with
> me as the lord of the manor and the person in whom the right of
> furnishing such supply is vested. The rights of the Charitable Society
> are expressly limited and confined to the particular springs demised to
> them, and from which they derive an income of £750 per annum. I do
> not feel that I am called upon to make any further sacrifice of the
> interests of myself and family…[147]

Donegall himself gave the impression that he would accept any reasonable compromise, and twice accepted terms which his son then turned down, but this may well have been good tactics. At a public meeting in 1838, when feeling about the matter was running pretty high in the town, the father was credited with 'kind, considerate, and cordial conduct in this affair, as on all former occasions when the interests of the town are concerned...'[148] Nevertheless it is quite clear that, no longer in a position to be magnanimous, the lord of the manor had been reduced to driving hard bargains with the citizens about a matter of vital interest to them in which he could play only a negative part. It was a similar story with attempts made by the Ballast Board to improve the harbour. The fact that the family had lost its political control of the town no doubt sharpened these conflicts.

7

DECLINE
AND FALL

THE PICTURE OF THE SECOND MARQUIS of Donegall that
emerges from the foregoing pages is a far from flattering one. The
financial difficulties in which he constantly found himself, and which
governed so much of his behaviour, were caused almost entirely either
by his own self-indulgence or by his evident lack of judgement and
common sense. And when, as so frequently happened, he got into
trouble by failing to listen to good advice, he appears to have been
none too scrupulous at times about evading his responsibilities, or at
the very least – since one is never quite sure to what extent he was being
used by others more intelligent and determined than himself – about
allowing his relations and advisers to act unscrupulously in his name.
Apparently he was both weak in character and also rather lacking in
principle. As Mrs McTier shrewdly observed, he was so easily exploited
by other people that one felt sorry for him, until he forfeited one's
sympathy by acting in just the same way himself towards those who
were foolish enough to trust him. The best that the charitable Benn
could say about him was that he 'did not possess the abilities of his
father; that while kind, benevolent, and always generous to the town,
he was destitute of that firmness of character, and that commanding
talent, necessary to deal with so great and rising a place as Belfast, or to
understand how to take equitable advantage of his position…'[149] In
other words, compared to his father Donegall was both weak and dim-
witted.

To some extent his great personal charm compensated for his short-
comings. Almost everyone who had anything to do with him liked his

easy manners and friendly nature. High rank and charming manners made a particularly strong impact on his social inferiors. A nobleman who was not only resident but also friendly and approachable was regarded as a distinct asset in local society, however much the successful merchants of Belfast may in their hearts have despised his inability to manage his affairs, an inability which in any case was very much to their advantage. In his latter years, Benn says, he was a familiar sight in the streets of the town, riding his white pony and attended only by a groom, and was on easy terms with many of the inhabitants. Dr Henry Cooke, the leading presbyterian divine, later recalled with evident pleasure that at a time when he himself had been ill Donegall had called every day to enquire after his health. Even presbyterian Belfast loved a lord.[150]

As head of a great family and patron of a couple of safe parliamentary seats he could not be denied recognition, whatever his deficiencies. Accordingly he was appointed to the Irish privy council in 1803, and was allowed to dispense most of the patronage of Belfast and Carrickfergus; the lucrative post of collector of customs for Belfast, for example, went to his brother-in-law Stephen May in 1816 on the death of Chichester Skeffington, who had got it by the patronage of the first marquis. The notoriety of his financial affairs, however, and the low personal esteem in which he was held in official circles, for long delayed his appointment to the Order of St Patrick, despite his anxiety to have it. The duke of Richmond (lord lieutenant of Ireland 1807-13) wrote to the home secretary in 1809: 'The marquis of Donegall has constantly asked for the ribbon [of the Order] but his having it would not be creditable.[151] He did eventually get it in 1821, one suspects partly as a gesture of sympathy in his matrimonial disaster. For the last dozen years of his life he represented the crown as lord lieutenant of County Donegal; characteristically, after a brief flurry of activity in the role when first appointed he became an indifferent absentee.[152]

He was much more active in local affairs. For causes and institutions of all kinds he was the indispensable patron, always willing to head a list or take the chair. Some of his appointments were formal ones inherited from his father, such as the presidency of the fever hospital and the Botanical Society. Among other things he was a governor of the lunatic asylum and a trustee of the Loan Society Fund (his lifetime's experience of borrowing may have helped him here). Steward at the Maze racecourse, commodore of the Belfast Yacht Club, president of the Northern Rowing Club and the Belfast Cricket Club, grand master of the local masons, patron of the Odd-Fellows – scarcely an activity of any kind established in Belfast during these years looked to him in vain.

His role with regard to local enterprises of a social and cultural kind is best illustrated in the early history of the Academical Institution. Though it later acquired royal approval, the Institution at its inception was regarded with suspicion by the government, as the proposal of the republican-minded citizens – 'the democratical establishment proposed at Belfast', as the future duke of Wellington, then Irish secretary, called it. Donegall and the elder May (as the local MP) exerted their influence to overcome the government's reluctance to give a grant. While Donegall's letter drew a polite official response, Wellesley's private note to Lord Liverpool about the matter revealed what its shrewd writer really thought of the promoters: 'Its patrons are Lord Donegall and Mr May. They, or rather the latter, has taken it up solely with a view of letting to advantage some ground at Belfast, of which he has a lease from Lord Donegall.'[153] From what we know of both men, there may well have been a good deal of substance in Wellesley's suspicions.

However, others had better reasons for wanting the project to proceed, and Donegall not only accepted the position of president for life but by doing so enlisted the support of Lord Downshire (a genuine enthusiast for education), the Honourable Edward Ward and William Brownlow, MP, all of whom – along with May – became vice-presidents. Donegall laid the foundation stone of the new Institution in July 1810 (the silver trowel which he used, now in the school's possession, he also used for the fever hospital in 1815, the Commercial Buildings in 1819 and the Gas Company's building in 1822 – an extraordinary instance of economy on someone's part) and took the chair at its opening in February 1814. To judge from his speech on that occasion he was perfectly capable of expressing the appropriate sentiments. 'Ever since I had the honour of laying the first stone of this building,' he said, 'I have watched its progress with the utmost pleasure and satisfaction; I am now most proud to see it so far advanced for the purpose intended…' After some good advice to the 'gentlemen teachers', the 'young gentlemen' and the directors and managers he concluded: 'Should my wishes be realised, I shall then flatter myself that I may see the Institution of this populous town rise triumphant over the heads of all others in this country.'[154] Such patronage was not only helpful but essential to the

Institution's success, as was the fee-farm grant of the ground on which it stood. Financial help was another matter: though Donegall's name headed the subscription list with the substantial sum of nearly £600, the money was never actually paid (nor did the Mays ever pay the sums they had promised). Since the managers of the Institution in those difficult early years equally failed to pay any rent, the arrears were eventually balanced against Donegall's subscription.[155]

It is clear from occasional glimpses in other collections of estate papers that the Donegalls enjoyed normal social relations with their aristocratic neighbours. When the marquis of Londonderry got news that the Russian grand duke was coming to the north of Ireland and intended to honour him with a visit to Mount Stewart, his first thought was to get up a suitable party. As he wrote to Castlereagh afterwards: 'Fortunately... we had time to send out all invitations and had our grand dinner prepared for his arrival on Thursday at four o'clock. We sat down to table twenty-nine in number: my wife on the right side of the royal duke, and Lady Donegall on the left. As she is very flippant [presumably he meant 'fluent'] in French and talking nonsense, she was of some use in helping to keep up the conversation...'[156] Her husband's failure to provide a reception in Belfast for the exotic visitor – which Londonderry pityingly ascribed to his being ashamed that he had neither the house nor the means – has been mentioned already. Londonderry was a new man, however, who managed his property with unusual thriftiness and efficiency and had not acquired a proper carelessness in such matters.

More revealing, because more typical, was the relationship between the Donegalls and the Downshires. Though originally clients of the Chichesters (their prophetically named ancestor Moses Hill had been a tenant of Sir Arthur Chichester before acquiring substantial property of his own), the Hills of Hillsborough had overtaken them in wealth and prestige and noble rank. The heads of both families became Irish marquesses and English peers in the late eighteenth century. The second marquis of Downshire had died comparatively young in 1801, leaving enormous debts and a boy of thirteen as his heir. The third marquis made it the object of his life, from 1809 until his death in 1845, to pay off his father's debts and do what his father had failed to do, by running his great property efficiently.[157] This solemn young man had little enthusiasm for horse-racing or gambling, and was the soul of probity in his financial affairs. Furthermore, the political interests of his family were usually opposed to those of the Donegalls in the borough of Carrickfergus. Yet class solidarity and the older man's charm were sufficient to overcome these differences, and the two appear to have been on friendly terms. They certainly called upon each other, and there is a letter from Donegall in the Downshire papers, dated December 1812, saying he has put Downshire's name down for a dinner of some sort in Belfast 'and you will make me particularly happy to dress at Donegall House on that day and take a bed and let me have the pleasure of going to the club with you'.[158] Even after Downshire's friends had tried to unseat the successful Donegall candidate at the election in Carrickfergus in 1812, Downshire was at pains to emphasise that no personal animosity was intended. 'I entertain every feeling of friendship and goodwill towards you…' he wrote, 'and any difference of opinion resulting from our property and our situation in life can only be local and cannot affect… that mutual intercourse and sociability… between your family and mine.'[159]

When the second marquis succeeded to the title and estates in 1799 the political influence of the Donegalls was considerable. Both of the members who represented Belfast in the Irish parliament, and one of the two for Carrickfergus, were invariably relatives or friends of the Chichesters, not to mention the family's influence in the elections for County Antrim. Donegall had been MP for Carrickfergus at the time of his succession, and his brother, who had been elected in both places, had represented Belfast. In Belfast the representation was entirely under the landlord's control, since the only voters were the twelve burgesses whom he appointed. By 1790 fewer than half of them were even residents of the town, for an act of 1748 and a judicial decision of ten years later had made it quite legal to elect non-residents as freemen and burgesses. The position in 1790 so far as Belfast was concerned was described by a hostile observer in this way:

> This residence of numerous, wealthy, and spirited inhabitants, remains in abject slavery to the absentee earl of Donegall; electing without enquiry whomsoever he nominates. It is indeed a *close* borough, that is, the election is made by twelve burgesses, nominated in effect, though not apparently, by his lordship, so that the inhabitants have no more influence in the choice of their representatives, than if they were sent over to them ready elected, by the worthy colony of Botany Bay.[160]

Accordingly Donegall nominated his father-in-law Edward May as one of the two MPs to represent the town in the last session of the Irish parliament, and May was its first single representative at Westminster after the parliaments were united. Stephen May succeeded his father in 1814 and, when he resigned in order to become collector of customs two years later, was followed as MP by Donegall's cousin Sir Arthur Chichester. Chichester in turn made way for the earl of Belfast when the young man came of age, and throughout the 1820s reverted to Carrickfergus, where he had been put in originally in 1812.

Since there was no possibility of an electoral contest in Belfast, little or no political management was required and there was no need to take political considerations into account when deciding to grant perpetuities in the town in the 1820s. The Reform Act of 1832 changed this state of affairs out of all recognition. Thereafter Belfast returned two members, elected by the more substantial citizens, who now not only had the franchise but also – since they were no longer dependent on Donegall for the continuation of their leases – the power to exercise it as they liked. An independent spirit had long existed, and had been increased by the agitation for parliamentary reform. When Sir Arthur Chichester, returned for Belfast in 1830 after losing at Carrickfergus to the Downshire candidate, put himself forward again in 1832 the newly formed Reform Society asked: 'What has our member, Sir Arthur Chichester, ever done for this town? He represents only the twelve burgesses. Where have we any record of his talents or his public exertions? No such record exists. He has done nothing for Belfast.'[161] After 1832, although two of Donegall's sons were indeed elected (Lord Arthur 1832–34 and Lord John 1845–52) they took their chance in public contests and stood on party platforms. In that first election for the reformed parliament, when Lord Arthur and James E. Tennent stood in the tory interest, the *Northern Whig* wrote of their campaign: 'My Lady Donegall has become wonderfully condescending. She has been visiting the tradesmen and shopkeepers in the town in the most captivating manner. What a farce!'[162] Whether farcical or not (the marquis had voted for the reform bill) it was certainly an extraordinary change from any previous Belfast election.

The loss of political control in parliamentary elections in Belfast was followed within a few years by the end of the family's monopoly in local government. Ever since 1613 the sovereign and burgesses had been appointed by the lord of the manor and had done his bidding, frequently to the dissatisfaction of the citizens, who with increasing wealth and numbers had been more and more inclined to help themselves by taking the initiative in improving the town. The rapid growth in the population of Belfast, from about 20,000 at the turn of the century to over 70,000 in 1841 – especially in the 1830s, when it rose by forty per cent to make the town twelfth in the United Kingdom – made its antique and unrepresentative administration increasingly indefensible; and the commission which investigated the Irish town corporations had no difficulty in deciding to recommend the replacement of the sovereign and burgesses by an elected council. Appropriately enough, the last man to hold the position of sovereign was Thomas Verner, Donegall's nephew and the son-in-law of Sir Edward May. When Verner failed to gain a seat in the elections for the new council in 1842, the aged Donegall burst into tears at a public meeting.[163]

Political control of the borough of Carrickfergus had always been a less straightforward matter, for the Donegalls owned only part of the town and independent interests always returned at least one of the two members and could on occasion threaten the Donegall candidate as well. There had been a notable instance in a by-election in the 1780s, when the Belfast merchant Waddell Cunningham was actually elected in defiance of the wishes of the fifth earl (as he then was) but was subsequently disqualified on petition to the House of Commons; and was defeated in a second contest only after fifty of his supporters had been disfranchised on dubious grounds. Cunningham had campaigned against the Donegall interest which, he said in his address to the electors, 'though not composed of more than a tenth part of the whole interests in your corporation, has ever endeavoured to trample on your rights, and oppose the objects of your choice; converting you into a venal borough, and disposing of you as private property.'[164] On the whole, however, there had been little difficulty in keeping control of one seat, so long as the admission of freemen was closely watched and the freemen themselves were wooed by the judicious use of Donegall's influence in obtaining government appointments for his supporters. After the defeat of Cunningham there was no trouble for the next twenty years, because the two seats were shared as before by tacit agreement (the mayoralty alternating) and because Donegall took care to recruit his following. As an observer remarked in 1790, since the days of Cunningham's challenge 'the absentee earl's interest had been much strengthened'.[165]

After 1800, however, when the representation of the town was reduced to a single seat, conflict was inevitable. The independent interests found a formidable leader in 1807 when the dowager marchioness of Downshire decided to further her political ambitions (she had earlier engineered the defeat of Castlereagh himself in a by-election for County Down) by buying the estate of the Lyndon family at Carrickfergus.[166]

Donegall himself foolishly assisted her plans by failing on this occasion to control the admission of new freemen – his financial difficulties and consequent enforced absence in Scotland may have contributed to his failure – and by choosing to put up as candidate his brother-in-law Edward May. The rival candidate, James Craig, defeated May in the two elections which were held in 1807, with the help of new voters. May petitioned the House of Commons after his defeat, but did not pursue the petition. Instead, he took legal proceedings against some of the new freemen and succeeded in disqualifying a number of them, while the new mayor in 1808 put out of the corporation the young marquis of Downshire, who had earlier been made an alderman though still under age. We know that May was regarded as quite unacceptable from the following letter written by Donegall to Downshire in 1812, when the challenge was renewed:

> As your lordship has mentioned Carrickfergus in your letter I am in-clined to mention my own feelings respecting it. In the great struggle that took place on a former occasion when an unnatural opposition was made to my father's interest in that corporation your father stood forward as the strenuous friend and supporter of our rights, which left the strongest affection on the minds of my family. I confess I enjoyed the hopes that it would have been continued on your part as it was then my most anxious wish that our interests should have gone to-gether and with that view I took the earliest opportunity of showing my zeal in the support of your family in the later contest with Lord Castlereagh and which I did with a perfect view of the justice of your claim on that occasion and I flattered myself that the same motive would have influenced you in Carrickfergus but to my surprise I expe-rienced an opposition to my hopes. I have since heard that not only the lady dowager but your lordship on several occasions have observed that the opposition was not meant towards me but to the then candi-date Mr Edward May. These objections have been effectually met [pre-sumably by dropping May in favour of Sir Arthur Chichester] not-withstanding which I experienced a similar opposition to my friend on the last contest.[167]

The truth was that though the Downshire challenge may have begun with objections to the person of Edward May it became the long-term aim to oust the Donegalls. Success was delayed for many years by a dispute over the title to the Lyndon estate, which was reckoned in 1826 to control fifty-six votes. It was delayed also by some assiduous management on the part of Donegall (or at any rate his advisers). The historian of Carrickfergus, Samuel McSkimin, writing in 1829 made this assessment of the situation:

> This corporation has been often represented as fully under the influence of the Chichester family; but it is certainly not subject to the control of any family or party. However, the marquis of Donegall has a very considerable influence, especially in the assembly, and many have free houses and lands from him, evidently for electioneering purposes. Of late years he has been extending his influence by dividing his lands here into smaller portions.[168]

The significance of that last remark is that Carrickfergus was the one part of the Donegall estates where the tenants were not offered perpetuities under the arrangement of 1822. The Donegall interest was also

Lord Donegall as an old man, with his groom, outside the Agricultural Bank in Belfast in 1843. This photograph in its original form was almost certainly the work of Francis Beatty, the pioneer of professional photography in Ireland, who had recently opened his studio in Castle Street.

maintained by the appointment of his supporters as revenue officers, tidewaiters and so on, and – even in times of great financial difficulty to himself – by generous subscriptions to public causes such as the fever hospital established in the hard years 1817–18. All this sounds competent enough. It was Downshire's strength, particularly financial strength, rather than Donegall's weakness that led to the loss of Carrickfergus. In 1830 McSkimin's remark that the town was not fully under the control of the Chichester family was proved true, when Lord Arthur Hill defeated Sir Arthur Chichester in the elections of that year. His other remark, that no family or party was in control, did not remain true for much longer, however. After Chichester had regained the seat he was disqualified on petition in 1833 and the borough was actually disfranchised for a few years. Thereafter for half a century it was under the undisputed control of the Downshires.

In the county of Antrim too, in which the Donegalls had such a large estate, the second marquis seems to have taken the necessary steps to influence his tenants to vote as he wished – at any rate in the early 1800s. The *Belfast News Letter* published the following notice in May 1806, the message of which is plain enough:

> To the gentlemen of the county of Antrim resident in and near Belfast–
>
> Gentlemen – A full conviction that the continuance of consequence, tranquillity and power to the British empire depends on the upright and unprejudiced choice of the members who sit in the Commons' House in parliament, makes me feel it my duty, as an independent proprietor of land in this kingdom, to request that the gentlemen who hold ground under me for terms of years will be so good as to call at my office in Belfast for the purpose of having a life added to each different lease [thus giving them votes]. I hope and trust that my ambition and vanity will be amply gratified by the sound and wise choice of representatives which you… will make when an opportunity offers… From my residence here and from the observations my understanding permits me to make, I am confident our objects and wishes will be the same – to preserve liberty and honest power in their greatest state of perfection.[169]

This influence was later sacrificed to financial expediency, however, for the greater part of the County Antrim estate was granted in perpetuities during the 1820s and therefore ceased to be amenable to the landlord's wishes.

By 1840, then, both the wealth and the power of the Donegalls had been seriously reduced, as a result partly of the second marquis's extravagance and incompetence, partly of developments beyond his control which tended to reduce or restrict the influence of landowners in general. By that time he himself was an old man, no longer in the best of health, and two of his sons were already dead. The youngest, Algernon, was engaged in reliving his father's youth in the clubs and gaming houses of London, being obliged to flee from his creditors (he went to Hamburg and eventually restored his fortunes by marrying a French countess).[170]

In the summer of 1844 Donegall became seriously ill and, when sea air was recommended by his doctors, moved to a cottage at Cultra. From there he returned in September to Ormeau, where he died early in October at the age of seventy-five.

The funeral was a great public occasion. By order of the town council all shops and businesses in Belfast were closed as a mark of respect. As the funeral procession made its way in the pouring rain through the town and on to the family vault at Carrickfergus it was accompanied by two hundred carriages and seen by thousands of spectators. The local newspaper did its best to mention everyone of importance in its account of the event:

> The physicians and clergy preceded the hearse, which was decorated with the heraldic bearings of the deceased, and the mourners, pall bearers, the corporation, boards of the Royal Academical Institution, Belfast corporation, members of the Belfast Academy, Natural History Society, Botanical Society, Linen Hall Committee, Antrim Militia, Constabulary, the members of the Society of Odd-Fellows wearing black silk scarfs, and their officers decorated with the insignia of the order, followed.[171]

Lord Donegall's final escape from his creditors quickly revealed the full extent of his extravagance. The enormous debts that he had left unpaid, after spending the money raised to pay them, added to those which his heir had contracted on his own account amounted to nearly £400,000, fourteen times the annual income. After attempts to sell portions of the estate privately had failed, the third marquis was obliged by the creditors to let the encumbered estates court sell the freehold of Belfast and some 30,000 acres in County Antrim in order to wipe the slate clean.[172] Somehow or other the second marquis had managed to postpone that reckoning and – often at other people's expense – to live like a lord all his life.

IN CHANCERY.

DONEGALL ESTATES.

NOTICE TO TENANTS.

JOHN TURNER AND OTHERS
v.
THE MARQUIS OF DONEGALL
AND OTHERS.

YOU are requested to TAKE NOTICE, that my Office will remain open for the Receipt of all RENTS and ARREARS of RENT, on each MONDAY, WEDNESDAY, and FRIDAY, from TEN to TWO o'clock, up to the 1st October. An early call to pay your year's Rent, due at May last, will much oblige: as

ALL TENANTS THEN ONE YEAR IN ARREAR WILL BE PROCEEDED AGAINST.

By Order,

THOMAS HUGHES, Receiver.

17, CASTLE CHAMBERS, 6th September, 1846.

The Donegall estate in Chancery, 1846. The spendthrift second marquis left enormous debts when he died in 1844, despite having raised the money to settle them. The creditors got a receiver appointed by the court of chancery and eventually forced the third marquis to part with the freehold of most of Belfast.

NMGNI ULSTER MUSEUM

NOTES

1. Charles Henry Talbot (1721–98) was the second son of Major-General Sheringham Talbot of Evesham. He was created an Irish baronet in 1790 through Donegall's influence.

2. The 'Castle' at this date consisted of some outbuildings of the castle destroyed by fire in 1708 which had been adapted as estate offices and a modest dwelling. This edifice lay in an extensive garden, behind the high wall of the old castle, bounded by Donegall Place, Castle Place and Castle Lane. When the second marquis of Donegall fled to Belfast in 1802, his law agent, Thomas Ludford Stewart, gave up his own house and moved into the Castle. Seventy years later, an elderly citizen could recall the long wall, overhung with old fruit trees, and the hawks and hounds kept by the sport-loving occupant.

3. [J.R.Scott], *The parliamentary representation of Ireland* (Dublin, 1790), p. 3.

4. See W.A. Maguire, 'Absentees, architects and agitators: the fifth earl of Donegall and the building of Fisherwick Park' in *Proceedings of Belfast Natural History and Philosophical Society*, second series, vol. 10 (1983), pp 5–21.

5. Haliday to Marchmont, 21 June 1788, quoted in G.E. C[ockayne], *Complete peerage*, iv (London, 1916), p. 392n.

6. Lady Newdigate-Newdegate, *The Cheverels of Cheverel Manor* (London, 1898), p. 121.

7. Printed papers in appeal from Irish court of chancery to House of Lords in *Houlditch and others v. Donegall*, 1830 (PRONI, D 1255/7/2/Box 234).

8. Copy settlement dated 19 May 1792 (PRONI, T 956/40).

9. Settlement dated 23 May 1794 (PRONI, D 389/29).

10. Grattan papers (PRONI transcript T 2007/Mic. 71 of Fitzwilliam/Langdale papers in Brynmor Jones Library, University of Hull).

11. See J. Ashton, *The Fleet: its river, prison and marriages* (London, 1889). When the reformer Howard visited the prison in 1776 there were 241 prisoners in the House and 78 in the Rules.

12. See B. Fitzgerald, *Lady Louisa Connolly, 1743–1821* (London, 1950), pp 155–7; and B. Fitzgerald (ed.), *Correspondence of Emily, Duchess of Leinster, 1731–1814* (3 vols, Dublin, 1949–57), ii, letters 153 and 154.

13. Lynch to Fitz-Gerald, 6 July 1791 (PRONI, Strutt papers, transcript T 3092/4).

14. *Mopia Kpateomenh… being a collection of all the addresses, squibs and songs, which appeared before, and at the Carrickfergus midsummer election, 1808* (Carrickfergus, 1808), p. 62.

15. Copy will dated 7 Aug. 1795 (PRONI, transcript, T 761/18).

16. Copy settlement dated 7 Aug. 1795 (Templemore papers, Dunbrody Park).

17. Appeal papers, 1830 (see 7 above).

18. Same.

19. Lyon to Skeffington, 11 Mar. 1802 (PRONI, Foster-Massereene papers, D 562/2852).

20. Lyon to Skeffington, 11 Nov. 1800 (same, 2901).

21. Same.

22. Donegall to Bernal, 10 July 1799 (Staffordshire County Record Office, M 521/4).

23. Donegall to Bernal, 30 September 1799 (same, M521/6).

24. Bernal to Donegall, 28 July 1800 (same).

25. Donegall to Bernal, 11 Nov. 1800 (same, M 521/4).

26. Donegall to Bernal, 23 Dec. 1800 (same).

27. May to Bernal, 11 Dec. 1800 (same, M 521/6).

28. May to Bernal, 13 Jan. 1801 (same).

29. May to Bernal, 31 Mar. 1801 (same).

30. May to Stevens, 18 Mar. 1802 (same).

31 May to Bernal, 15 Apr. 1802 (same).

32 Lyon to Skeffington, early 1802 (PRONI, Foster-Massereene papers, D 562/2848).

33 Lyon to Skeffington, 22 Mar. 1802 (same, 2851).

34 Lyon to Skeffington, 11 Mar. 1802 (same, 2852).

35 McTier to W. Drennan, 8 Mar. 1802. *The Drennan-McTier Letters*, ed. Jean Agnew (3 vols, Dublin, 1998–9), iii, p. 18.

36 McTier to S. Drennan, 10 Apr. 1802 (same, iii, p. 34).

37 McTier to W. Drennan, 10 Apr. 1802 (same, iii, p. 35).

38 PRONI, transcript T 1565.

39 McTier to W. Drennan, 3 June 1802 (*Letters*, iii, p. 48).

40 McTier to W. Drennan, ?15 Dec. 1806 (same, iii, p. 549).

41 McTier to W. Drennan, June 1802 (same, iii, p. 48).

42 McTier to S. Drennan, 23 Jan. 1803 (same, iii, p. 101).

43 McTier to W. Drennan, [ ] Jan. 1806 (same, iii, p. 414).

44 Lyon to Skeffington, 8 Mar. 1803 (PRONI, Foster-Massereene papers, D 562/2806).

45 McTier to W. Drennan, 4 June 1803 (*Letters*, iii, p. 114).

46 PRONI, D 509/1517, dated 4 Nov. 1803.

47 McTier to W. Drennan, [ ] Jan. 1806 (*Letters*, iii, p. 414).

48 McTier to W. Drennan, 11 Mar. 1805 (same, iii, p.331).

49 It was apparently common knowledge that the Mays had their eye on this valuable living, which was in the gift of Donegall, for an amusing Carrickfergus election squib of 1808 related their premature rejoicing after a false report of the death of the incumbent (*Mopia Kpateomenh*, pp 63–4).

50 McTier to W. Drennan, 19 Dec. 1806 (*Letters*, iii, p. 548).

51 McTier to S. Drennan, 1 Mar.1806 (same, iii, p. 435).

52 McTier to W. Drennan, 5 Jan. 1807 (same, iii, p. 555).

53 William Todd of Buncrana Castle was the survivor of a fatal duel, fought with a neighbour named Hartley near Buncrana in 1810. See H.P. Swan, *The book of Inishowen* (Buncrana, 1938), p. 42.

54 G. Benn, *A history of the town of Belfast* (2 vols., London, 1877–80), ii, pp 63–4.

55 Staffordshire County Record Office, M521/6, undated but c.1816.

56 Benn, *Belfast*, ii, p. 56.

57 J. Dubourdieu, *Statistical survey of the county of Antrim* (2 vols., London, 1812), ii, p. 325.

58 PRONI, D 2977.

59 R. Mortimer, *The history of the Derby stakes* (London, 1962), pp 7–8. See also J.B. Priestley, *The prince of pleasure and his regency* (London, 1969), p. 46.

60 Archibald Hamilton Rowan at one time employed Jack as coachman at his place near Hounslow Heath and suspected that some of his hunters had been out at night (see *Autobiography*, ed. W.M. Drummond (Dublin, 1840), pp 36–7).

61 See petition cited in no. 58 above.

62 Same.

63 Richard Wolseley, born in 1760, was curate of the parish of Drumbo near Belfast in 1808. A crony of Donegall's, he had been made a burgess of the corporation. He married three times, inherited a baronetcy and lived to be over ninety.

64 See petition cited in no. 58 above.

65 Quoted in R.D.C. Black, *Economic thought and the Irish question, 1817–70* (Cambridge, 1960), p. 19.

66 Copy will dated 7 Aug. 1795, with codicils of 22 Nov. 1798 and 29 Dec. 1798 (PRONI, T 761/18).

67 Camden to Portland, 2 Jan. 1798 (PRO London, Home Office papers 100, vol. 70, ff. 325–7).

68 See A.P.W. Malcomson, *The extraordinary career of the 2nd earl of Massereene, 1743–1805* (Belfast, HMSO, 1972), pp 35–6.

69 See P.W. Clayden, *Rogers and his contemporaries* (2 vols., London, 1889), i, pp 22–3.

70 Donegall to Skeffington, 31 August 1806 (PRONI, Foster-Massereene papers, D 562/2818).

71 Donegall to Donegall, 10 Sept. 1806 (same, 2828).

72 Donegall to Skeffington, 23 Sept. 1805 (same, 2817).

73 Donegall to Skeffington, 17 Oct. 1806 (same, 1942).

74 Donegall to Skeffington, 17 Oct. 1806 (same, 1942).

75 Donegall to Skeffington, 24 Oct. 1806 (same, 2894).

76 Donegall to Skeffington, 3 Nov. 1806 (same, 2829).

77 Donegall to Skeffington, 12 Feb. 1808 (same, 2820).

78 Donegall to Skeffington, 2 Oct. 1808 (same, 2821).

79 Donegall to Skeffington, 2 Oct. 1808 (same, 2821).

80 Donegall to Skeffington, 28 Nov. 1808 (same, 2819).

81 Donegall to Skeffington, 30 Jan. 1809 (same, 2822).

82 Donegall to Skeffington, 10 May 1810 (same, 2823).

83 Donegall to Skeffington, 24 May 1810 (same, 2824).

84 Donegall to Skeffington, 22 June 1810 (same, 2825).

85 Donegall to Skeffington, 8 July 1810 (same, 2826).

86 Donegall to Skeffington, Aug. (?) 1810 (same, 2831).

87 R. Mortimer, *The Jockey club* (London, 1958), p. 21; and *The history of the Derby stakes* (London, 1962), pp 7–8.

88 Grattan papers, as at no. 10 above.

89 Cornwall to Faulkner, 10 and 24 Feb. 1791 (National Library of Ireland, transcript of Faulkner papers).

90 Cornwall to Faulkner, 4 June 1792 (same).

91 Malcomson, *Massereene*, p. 33.

92 O'Kelly to 'W.W.', 26 Sept. 1794 (Grattan papers, as at no. 10 above).

93 Lady Donegall to O'Kelly, 1 Sept. 1800 (same).

94 O'Kelly to Lady Donegall, 4 Sept. 1800 (same).

95 Anon to Lady Donegall, no date (same).

96 Appeal papers in *Donegall and others v. Grattan and Grattan*, c.1830 (PRONI, D 1255/7/2, Box 234).

97 Same.

98 Same.

99 Same.

100 Harvey to Hertford, 21 Dec. 1813 (PRONI, Hertford papers, transcript T 3076/2/59).

101 Harvey to Hertford, 3 Mar. 1815 (same, 66).

102 'P. O'K.' to O'Kelly, 22 Aug. 1817 (Grattan papers, as at no. 10 above).

103 Same.

104 Appeal papers in *Grattan v. Donegall* dated 15 Jan. 1846 (PRONI, D 971/5/5A (Box 57)).

105 G.E.C., *Peerage*, iv, p. 392, n.

106 Same, p. 392.

107 Palmerston to Temple, 16 July 1819 (Templemore papers at Dunbrody Park).

108 Appendix to *Chronicle*, p. 292.

109 Quoted in E. Hodder, *The life and work of the seventh earl of Shaftesbury* (2 vols, London, 1886), i, p. 51.

110 W.P. Eversley, *Law of domestic relations* (sixth ed., London, 1951), p. 15.

111 *Hansard*, second series, vol. vi, col. 1326n.

112 Legal opinion dated 24 Dec. 1821 (PRONI, D 971/5/5A, Box 57).

113 See no. 104 above.

114 S. Millin, *Sidelights on Belfast history* (Belfast and London, 1932), p. 44.

115 *Hansard*, vi, cols. 1360–1n.

116 *Belfast News Letter*, 19 Oct. 1819.

117 Harvey to Hertford, 11 Oct. 1819 (PRONI, transcript T 3076/2/75 of Hertford papers (Egerton MSS) in the British Library).

118 Same.

119 Same.

120 Deposition of Mary Hyde Mundy, 12 Feb. 1821 (PRONI, D 389/37).

121 Deposition of Elizabeth Verner, 4 Apr. 1821 (same).

122 3 Geo. IV, c. 75.

123 *Hansard*, vi, cols. 1326–62.

124 *Hansard*, vii, col. 1455.

125 Arthur Chichester's diary reveals the extent of his efforts to defeat the retrospective clause (Templemore papers, Dunbrody Park).

126 *Hansard*, vii, col. 1643.

127 Same, col. 1645.

128 Same, col. 1639.

129 Same, cols. 1635–6.

130 Same, col. 1647.

131 Eversley, *Law of Domestic Relations*, pp 15–16.

132 See no. 116 above.

133 PRONI, transcript T 956/61. For a detailed analysis see W.A. Maguire, 'The 1822 settlement of the Donegall estates' in *Irish Economic and Social History*, 3 (1976), pp 17–32.

134 *Report… into the state of the law and practice in respect of the occupation of land in Ireland* (4 vols., Dublin, 1845), i, p. 13.

135 Downshire to Reilly, 4 May 1833 (PRONI, Downshire papers, printed in W.A. Maguire (ed.), *Letters of a great Irish landlord* (HMSO, Belfast, 1974), pp 165–6.

136 J. Boyle, *Ordnance Survey notes for the parish of Donegore* (published with notes and additions by Queen's University, Belfast and PRONI, Belfast, 1974), p. 12.

137 Benn, *Belfast*, ii, p. 141.

138 PRONI, D 971/5/5A (Box 57).

139 Londonderry to Castlereagh, 24 Aug. 1818 (PRONI, Castlereagh papers, D 3030/H/40).

140 For the history of Ormeau and an analysis of Macartney's accounts, see W.A. Maguire, 'Ormeau House' in *Ulster Journal of Archaeology* 3rd series, vol. 42 (1979), pp 66–71 and 'A resident landlord in his local setting: the second marquis of Donegall at Ormeau' in *Proceedings of the Royal Irish Academy*, vol. 83 C, no. 15 (1983).

141 See note 135 above.

142 Donegall to Macrory, 6 Aug. 1836, quoted in R.W.M. Strain, *Belfast and its Charitable Society* (Oxford, 1961), p. 237.

143 [Pierce Egan], *Real Life in Ireland… by A Real Paddy* (London, 1904, reprint of 4th edition, pp 14–15. The author was well-informed about Donegall's (Done-'em-all's) history and reputation, as the following passage shows:

This man in early life dissipated an immense sum of money, besides a handsome annual allowance from an indulgent father; he was a *flat* among *sharps*. They *stagged* him in every corner, stuck to him like *fogle-hunters* [handkerchief thieves, such as the boys of Fagin's gang in *Oliver Twist*], eased him of the *jingling Georgy's* and lodged him in the College of

Insolvents. There he was boarded by a *land-shark*, a sort of *May*-day lawyer, who contrived to compromise with his creditors, and cheat them in doing so, and also to cheat him by whom he was employed. The young Lord paid the price of his person to gain his liberty, and made himself a slave for life – he married the lawyer's daughter.

144 Strain, *Charitable Society*, pp 212–235.

145 Same, p. 237.

146 Same, p. 236.

147 Same, p. 219.

148 Same, p. 226.

149 Benn, *Belfast*, ii, p. 12.

150 *Belfast News Letter*, 22 Oct. 1844.

151 Richmond to Ryder, 4 Dec. 1809 (PRONI, transcript T 33228/4/4 of Harrowby MSS, Vol. xciv, f. 156).

152 He visited County Donegal in February 1832 in order to investigate disturbances in the barony of Inishowen (where his own estates were) and in the Ballyshannon area. His copy letter book contains a dozen letters to Dublin Castle about his findings, but by 20 February he was back at Ormeau and the only subsequent entries in the book are recipes for such things as rat poison, turtle soup and the treatment of distemper in dogs. The volume is in the possession of the Central Reference Library, Belfast, and I am indebted to Mr John Gray for bringing it to my attention.

153 Quoted in J.R. Fisher and J.H. Robb, *The book of the Royal Belfast Academical Institution* (Belfast, 1913), p. 40.

154 Same.

155 J. Jamieson, *The history of the Royal Belfast Academical Institution, 1810–1960* (Belfast, 1959), p. 3.

156 Londonderry to Castlereagh, 24 Aug. 1818 (PRONI, Castlereagh papers, D 3030/H/40).

157 See W.A. Maguire, *The Downshire estates in Ireland, 1801–1845* (Oxford, 1972).

158 Donegall to Downshire, 20 Dec. 1812 (PRONI, Downshire papers, D 671/C/12/131).

159 Downshire to Donegall, 22 Dec. 1813 (same, 137).

160 [J.R. Scott], *The parliamentary representation of Ireland* (Dublin, 1790), pp 4–5.

161 Quoted in D.G. Owen, *History of Belfast* (Belfast, 1911), p. 256.

162 Same, p. 257.

163 *Northern Whig*, 25 Oct. 1842.

164 S. Millin, *Sidelights on Belfast history*, pp 39–40.

165 Scott, *Parliamentary Representation*, p. 9.

166 Maguire, *Downshire Estates*, pp 10–11.

167 Donegall to Downshire, 24 Nov. 1812 (PRONI, Downshire papers, D 671/C/12/130).

168 S. M'Skimin, *The history and antiquities of Carrickfergus* (3rd ed., Belfast, 1829), p. 202. I am grateful to Mrs Sheela Speers for letting me read her unpublished thesis on Carrickfergus which analyses the various interests in the corporation.

169 *Belfast News Letter*, 16 May 1806.

170 PRONI, Donegall letters, D 1798.

171 *Belfast News Letter*, 15 Oct. 1844.

172 See W.A. Maguire, 'Lord Donegall and the Sale of Belfast: a case history from the encumbered estates court', in *Economic History Review*, second series, vol. xxix, no. 4 (Nov., 1976), pp 570–584.

INDEX